First People

First People

The Early Indians of Virginia

SECOND EDITION

Keith Egloff and Deborah Woodward

Published in association with the VIRGINIA DEPARTMENT OF HISTORIC RESOURCES

UNIVERSITY OF VIRGINIA PRESS
Charlottesville and London

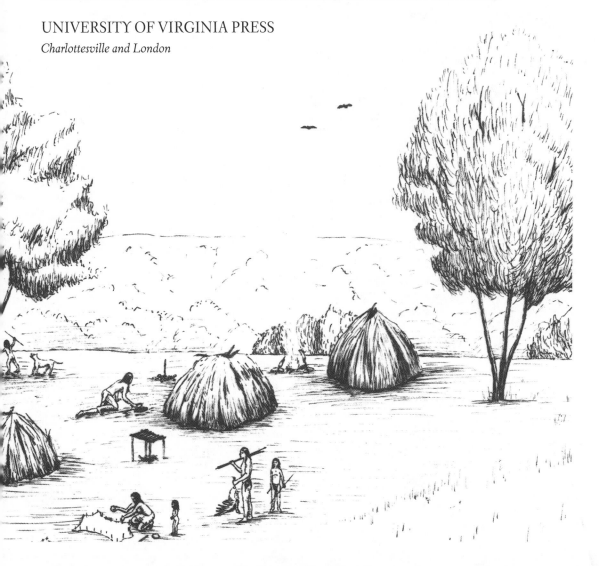

This volume was created in cooperation with the Jefferson National Forest–USDA Forest Service.

Illustrations, unless otherwise noted, are from the collections of the Virginia Department of Historic Resources.

University of Virginia Press
© 1992, 2006 by the Virginia Department of Historic Resources
All rights reserved
Printed in the United States of America on acid-free paper

First edition published 1992. Second edition published 2006.

9 8 7 6 5 4

LIBRARY OF CONGRESS CATALOGING-IN-PUBLICATION DATA
Egloff, Keith.
    First people : the early Indians of Virginia / Keith Egloff and Deborah Woodward. — 2nd ed.
        p.   cm.
    Includes bibliographical references and index.
    ISBN-13: 978-0-8139-2548-6 (pbk. : alk. paper)
    1. Indians of North America—Virginia. I. Woodward, Deborah (Deborah B.) II. Title.
    E78.V7E37 2006
    975.5'01—dc22

                                    2006004630

Title page illustration: Early hunters. (By Thomas Whyte; courtesy of the Frank H. McClung Museum, The University of Tennessee)

Cover illustration: by Theodor de Bry, the engraver and publisher of a four-language edition of Thomas Hariot's *A briefe and true report of the new found land of Virginia* (1590). De Bry's engravings were based on the paintings of John White, governor of the 1587 colony to Roanoke Island and an artist who painted the people and places he encountered in what is now coastal North Carolina. The engraving depicts a portion of the palisaded town of Pomeiooc. The image offers a good example of artistic license. In general, de Bry's engraving conforms to White's painting, with a number of minor differences. However, from recent archaeological evidence, researchers know that houses were built with rounded and not flat ends, as depicted by White. Also, there is no evidence for the colorful red roofs. (Illustration from the Collections at the Library at The Mariners' Museum, Newport News, Virginia)

Contents

Foreword

First People: The Early Indians of Virginia originally appeared in 1992 under the imprint of the Virginia Department of Historic Resources, the fulfillment of a longtime goal of the agency made possible at last by support from the Jefferson National Forest–USDA Forest Service. In the years since, and through successive printings by the University of Virginia Press, the book has been a publishing success. Readers of all kinds—students and scholars, teachers and tourists, from around the Commonwealth, the country, and the globe—have consistently kept the book sold out, showing an eagerness to learn about Virginia Indians. With this redesigned and updated edition, *First People* is again available as a concise and readable narrative. Its release not only satisfies a need; it is perfectly timed just ahead of the 400th anniversary of the founding of Jamestown to underscore that Virginia history did not begin in 1607.

Interest and receptivity were not always the case. Indeed, through much of the twentieth century, Virginia Indians faced a struggle to retain and recapture their cultural identity. As the text reminds us, for nearly fifty years prior to 1972, Virginia policies and laws attempted to obliterate Indians through "documentary genocide" in vital records.

At work as well were, and still are, less dramatic but insidious popular cultural forces that stand in the way of broad awareness of Virginia Indians' place in history and their strength as living people. Thus, the power of real history to inform, inspire, and teach has been weakened by persistent Disney-like myths, and the diverse cultures of Virginia Indians, along with those of other Eastern Woodland Native Americans, eclipsed and confused with images of the American West and Plains Indians. Thus, too, even at home in Virginia, citizens are often surprised to learn of the very existence of a modern-day and dynamic Virginia Indian community in the Commonwealth.

Thankfully, in recent decades the Commonwealth has made great strides in according Virginia Indians the respect and recognition that is their due and right. As well, the Virginia Indian community and scholars have nurtured a dialogue that enriches both communities and adds to our knowledge and understanding. This new edition is the fruit of a continuing partnership in the spirit and the hope of that dialogue. It is at heart a reflection of the Department's commitment and honor to listen and learn, and to work with Virginia Indians to help spread their stories. We trust the reader will find in *First People* an open door to the rich world of Virginia Indians, past and present.

Kathleen S. Kilpatrick
Director, Department of Historic Resources

Acknowledgments

First People has enjoyed widespread popularity in the public schools and the Indian and archaeological communities of Virginia since it was first conceived and brought to publication in 1992 by the Virginia Department of Historic Resources. This updated second edition incorporates recent events in the Indian community as well as additional information gleaned from publications and public resources that were not available more than a decade ago. It also reflects the commitment of the department, under the guidance of its director, Kathleen S. Kilpatrick, to tell the stories representing the full diversity of Virginia's rich history, without whose support this revised edition would not be possible. The authors would also like to recognize the timely and thorough review of this edition by Karenne Wood (Monacan), chair, and Deanna Beacham, program specialist, both of the Virginia Council on Indians.

The writing of the first edition was a collaboration of the authors—as staff of the Department of Historic Resources—and the Virginia Indian community. Many people and organizations deserve our heartfelt thanks and continued recognition for their contributions: Mary Ellen Hodges, who nurtured the original idea of the manuscript; the Council of Virginia Archaeologists' Education Committee, which saw the need for the book; Mike Barber, Jefferson National Forest, who made the writing of the manuscript possible; Archeological Society of Virginia members Howard MacCord, the late Sandra Speiden, and Martha Williams; and Catherine Slusser, whose guidance and support made the first edition possible.

We would also like to acknowledge the late Chief Webster Custalow for his vision and wisdom, Gary Flowers, Daniel Fortune, Paula Barnes, the late Chief Emeritus Earl Bass, Mitchell L. Bush Jr., Warren Cook, Dr. Linwood Custalow, the late John Sun Eagle, Jeffrey Hantman, Phyllis Hicks, Joan Johnson, Faye Fortune, Mike Lovings, Shirley Custalow McGowan, H. Bryan Mitchell, Chief Emeritus Oliver Perry for his steadfast support, Margaret T. Peters, Dennis Pogue, Ted Reinhart, Doug Price, Doug Sanford, E. Randolph Turner III, Chief Ken Adams, Chief Stephen Adkins, and especially Chief Emeritus Raymond S. Adams, Mr. and Mrs. Moses Adams, the late Chief Emeritus Arthur L. Adkins, Gary Bond, Chief Marvin Bradby, Birdie Sours, Judy Fortune, Donald Keith Lewis Sr., and Chief William Miles. For their work on the current edition, we also thank Randall Jones at the Department of Historic Resources and, at the University of Virginia Press, Ellen Satrom, managing editor, Gary Kessler, copy editor, and Martha Farlow, design and production manager.

I am pleased that in the past decades there has been increased collaboration between academics such as historians, anthropologists, and archaeologists and the Virginia Indians. However, it is important that nonnative scholars not try to tell the stories of the native people, but instead let the Indians speak for themselves. As with First People, *true collaboration happens only when enlightened academics ask indigenous people for their opinions and perspectives and report them as expressed, rather than trying to speak from an Indian point of view. Our views are influenced by the stories told to us by our elders as well as by our own experiences.*
—CHIEF EMERITUS OLIVER L. PERRY, NANSEMOND INDIAN TRIBE

Wingapo
Welcome

In the early 1600s, an English sea captain, while talking to a native chief along the coast of Virginia, was told this story of creation (modern translation by the Jamestown-Yorktown Foundation, from William Strachey, *The Historie of Travell into Virginia Britania*):

The Great Hare

The chief of all the gods was a Great Hare, and he dwelt in a place toward the rising sun.

The Great Hare thought how he wanted to people the earth. He made many different kinds of men and women, but he put them all into a very large bag.

Some giants came to visit the Great Hare. When they discovered what was in the bag, they wanted to eat all the people for a fine feast. The Great Hare was so angry at these cannibals that he drove the giants away from his house.

The godlike Hare went about making the water and filling it with fish. He made the land and placed upon the land a great deer to feed from the land.

Now, there were four lesser gods who were the four winds seated at each corner of the world. They were jealous of the deer sharing their land. They fashioned hunting poles, which they used to kill the great deer. After they dressed the meat and had a delicious feast, they departed to their four corners.

When the Great Hare saw what jealousy had caused, he took up the hairs of the slain deer and scattered them over the earth, chanting many powerful words and charms. Every tiny hair became a new deer.

Then the Great Hare opened the bag that held the men and the women. He placed a man and a woman upon the earth in one country and a man and a woman in another country. And so the world became filled with many different kinds of people.

Introduction

In Search of the Indians of Virginia

Most of what we know about the first people of Virginia has come from studying traces of the villages, mounds, cave shelters, and objects they left behind. Through patient work, archaeologists have reconstructed some of the history and lifeways of these first people. A clear picture of how Indian cultures in Virginia changed through time emerges from these findings.

Many people wonder how archaeologists can piece together the story of a people who left no written records—a people who communicated without a written language. Perhaps this behind-the-scenes look will help explain how scientists reached the account presented in this book.

The Daugherty's Cave Site in Southwest Virginia dates from 8000 BC to AD 1600. Archaeologists excavating the rockshelter carefully dug and sifted the soil through a fine screen to recover groups of artifacts found just as the Indians had left them. A small circle of black earth filled with pieces of rock and pottery, animal bones, and mussel, snail,

Map of Virginia shows the rivers, valleys, and mountainous regions in which the first people settled for over 15,000 years. Note the location of prominent tribes at the time of contact with European settlers in the 1600s.

and walnut shells revealed a fireplace, or hearth, around which the first people cooked and lived long ago. Near the hearth, the archaeologists found stone tools that were used to cut meat, scrape and pierce animal skins, and carve wood and bone.

Digging deeper, they came upon another hearth at a deeper level, or stratum, that held more clues. They found stone tools, animal bones, and charred hickory shells, but no pottery, at this second hearth. Delving deeper through the stratigraphy, the archaeologists found only stone tools. The lowest strata contained the oldest artifacts. The tools from the two hearths differed so much that the archaeologists believed they came from two distinct cultures, separated by long periods of time.

How old were the two hearths and associated objects? Physicists have learned to tell the age of charred wood by a technique called radiocarbon dating. This technique compares the amount of radioactive carbon ($C14$) to regular carbon ($C12$) in the pieces of organic material that was once alive, such as wood, bone, or shell. This process gives an age in calendar years and is an absolute dating technique. The charred wood from the upper hearth was found to date to AD 322, and from the lower hearth, to 3740 BC. Objects found near the hearths, in the same layer, share similar dates.

With one small excavation, the archaeologists learned a lot about two cultures separated by 4,000 years. The research often raised more questions than it answered, and other sites must be studied to recover other pieces to the puzzle.

The objects from Daugherty's Cave were saved for study. Preserved and stored, they joined other artifacts in the collection of the Virginia Department of Historic Resources. This immense collection contains material from many sites across Virginia, dating from 15,000 BC to the 19th century.

Most of what we have learned about the first people at Daugherty's Cave came after objects were unearthed at the site and studied in the lab. Scientists from different fields of specialty pored over them, and from each of their findings, we now know about the plants, animals, and rocks the first people used for food and tools.

Archaeologists have learned that Indians of the same culture at any one time almost always made their tools in a similar way. As time passed, the shapes of stone artifacts and the decorations on pottery changed. Material items, then, did not remain the same—they changed in response to the needs and desires of the people. Change occurred slowly or quickly. Normally, the greater the contact between two cultures, the faster their material items changed.

The archaeologists used studies of living cultures to interpret groups of the past, in a process called analogy. They looked to reports by cultural anthropologists, based on human groups untouched by the modern world. These included tribes found in remote areas of South America, Africa, Australia, and New Guinea. The social structure, shelter, food ways, economy, and technology of several of these cultures were then compared to those of the early Indians of Virginia. The archaeologists also used ethnohistory, the study of native groups through written records, to learn about the Indians after the first visits of Europeans to Virginia. These records give us views of Indian life from the perspective of the earliest European explorers, settlers, and traders.

Pamahsawuh

The Created World and Everything in It

"The People": What the Indians Called Themselves

Our natural environment is a dynamic place in which change is one of the few real constants. What is our role between earth and sky? What strategies can we use that will sustain us and our earth? Sometime before 15,000 BC Asians stood at the brink of a new land that was pristine, uninhabited, virgin. They crossed the largest frontier ever traveled. As one scientist observed, "not until the human race occupies another planet will we explore a domain so vast." Before the Pyramids were built in Egypt, before Greece enjoyed its Golden Age, before the Great Wall of China was laid, these people journeyed to the outermost reaches of the territory before them. From the Bering Strait, through Canada, and across the Great Plains, they arrived in Virginia long before there was even a Chesapeake Bay. Here, they adapted over many generations to changing environments, responding to their world and finding that it, in turn, responded to them.

They lived with nature and adapted their lifestyles to their surroundings and the seasons. From scientific findings, we know they dealt with years of drought, glacial advances, and retreats; the birth of a vast bay, rivers, and forests; the death of huge herd animals such as the mastodons and mammoths. By analogy with similar groups living today, we can assume the people believed all things had life and spirit—people, animals, water, wind, sun, moon, sky, rocks, and plants. They made all the tools and materials needed to sustain themselves. They invented atlatls, pottery, and celts. They learned to use plants to create containers, handles, fish weirs, cloth, medicine, housing, and canoes. They hunted animals for food, tools, shelter, and clothing.

The descendants of these first people were members of distinct

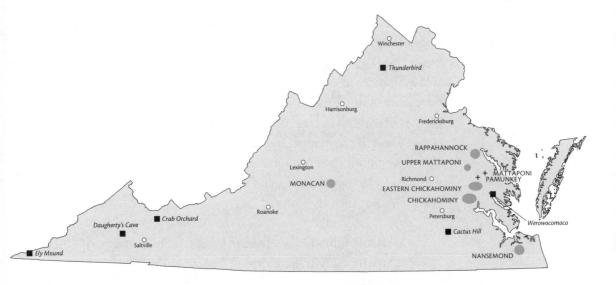

Map showing location
of Virginia Indians reservations and communi-
ties today, also impor-
tant archaeological sites,
such as Thunderbird,
Daugherty's Cave, Crab
Orchard, Ely Mound,
Cactus Hill, and Wero-
wocomoco.

tribes, speaking many different languages and dialects and holding many different beliefs and traditions. Each village was the center of a person's life. Tribal spheres of influence stretched as villages formed and broke alliances and established networks for trade. From 15,000 BC to AD 1600, the Indians of Virginia underwent a transformation from nomadic hunters to settled village farmers, from equal partners in small bands to members of elaborately organized chiefdoms.

What were their patterns and strategies for survival? How did they relate to each other? How did they respond to their world and its continual call for change? Oliver L. Perry, chief emeritus, Nansemond Tribe, and board member of the National Governor's Interstate Indian Council, expresses the wisdom of the Virginia Indian perspective simply: "Live in harmony with Mother Earth and Father Sky . . . Native Americans did and still do believe in the strength and value of family: Honor your ancestors. Respect your elders. Love, protect, and educate your children. They are the future—ours and yours."

At the height of their population, an estimated 50,000 Indians lived in Virginia at thousands of sites along waterways and the coast. Today, about 3,500 people of Indian ancestry reside in Virginia as members of state-recognized tribes. Their names are entered on the tribal register with their solemn pledge to uphold the traditions of the tribe. Census figures hold that 25,118 more people of American Indian, Alaskan, and Hawaiian ancestry live in urban areas, such as Tidewater, Northern

Virginia, Roanoke, and Richmond. Many of the Indians of Northern Virginia are enrolled members of tribes outside Virginia. They also belong to local Indian clubs, one of which, the American Indian Society of Washington, has purchased and maintains a 46-acre wooded tract in Caroline County. Eight organized groups together make up one of the largest populations of Indians on the East Coast. These include the Pamunkey and the Mattaponi, two tribes in King William County. Their state reservations date from the 1600s. Six other incorporated groups are officially recognized as Indian tribes by the Commonwealth of Virginia. They are the:

- Chickahominy Indian Tribe in Charles City County;
- Chickahominy Indian Tribe—Eastern Division in New Kent County;
- Monacan Indian Nation in Amherst County;
- Nansemond Indian Tribe in the City of Chesapeake;
- Rappahannock Indian Tribe in Essex, Caroline, and King and Queen counties;
- and the Upper Mattaponi Indian Tribe in King William County.

The two reservation Indian groups have maintained their tribal identity throughout the course of their history. Since their treaty of 1677, they have been recognized and treated as wards of the Commonwealth. The nonreservation communities began reorganizing into their tribal identities of origin in the late 1800s. In the last hundred years, new self-images have emerged among the people as they arrived at a balance of the old and the new in their lives. After enduring nearly four hundred years of exclusion and attempts to destroy their way of life, they struggle even now to rid themselves of the widespread misunderstandings that pervade our culture. They are picking up the threads of old traditions in their lives in ways that give them renewed meaning. To understand who they are, and how they have survived, we have to go back to the very beginning.

A Chronology of Virginia Indian and Old World Events

Old World Event	Time Period	Stage of Development	Cultural Period	Environment	Subsistence Pattern	Social Group/Settlement	Material Culture
European Upper Paleolithic	15,000–8000 BC	Early hunters	Paleoindian	Cold & moist: sedges, grasses, spruce, fir, pine	Hunting, supplemented by general gathering	Bands/Encampments	Stone fluted points, scrapers, flake tools, wedges, gravers, drills, hammerstones
Old World domestication of plants & animals	8000–6000 BC		Early Archaic	Warmer & drier: pine, spruce, fir, oak, birch, beech			Additions: side- & corner-notched points
	6000–2500 BC	Dispersed foragers	Middle Archaic	Warmer & moister: oak, pine, hemlock	Diversification of hunting & gathering	Band clusters/Encampments	Additions: atlatl stones, axes, pestles & mortars, net sinkers, increased use of bone scrapers and awls
Neolithic Bronze Age	2500–1200 BC		Late Archaic	Very warm & dry: oak, hickory, chestnut, pine	Intensified hunting & gathering, with introduction of cultigens (gourd & squash)	Transition to tribes/Hamlets	Additions: soapstone vessels; shell ornaments; bone needles, pins, & fishhooks; copper artifacts
Shang Dynasty Stonehenge King Solomon	1200–500 BC	Sedentary foragers	Early Woodland				Additions: ceramic vessels & pipes Additions: stone burial mounds, celt, bow & arrow
Alexander the Great	500 BC–AD 900		Middle Woodland	Cooler & moister: oak, chestnut, pine, hickory			
Mohammed	AD 900–1600	Farmers	Late Woodland	Modern conditions	Intensified hunting & gathering, with dependency on cultigens (corn, beans, squash, & tobacco)	Tribes or chiefdoms/Villages	Additions: earthen burial mounds, substructure mounds, pictographs
Henry VII Columbus Shakespeare	AD 1600		Historic		Introduction of European cultigens & domesticated animals	Population reduction, relocation, & consolidation with European expansion	Additions: European ornamentation, tools, & household items

Early Hunters

With the Indians, there were no fences, no boundaries.
The land was there for everyone to enjoy.
—Earl Bass, Running Deer, Chief Emeritus,
  Nansemond Indian Tribe

Paleoindian Period, 15,000–8000 BC

Scientists today do not agree on when people originally entered the Western Hemisphere. Many believe that by 15,000 BC the first people entered North America from Asia over land that connected present-day Siberia and Alaska at the end of the last great ice age (the Pleistocene). People crossed over a wide land bridge that resulted from a cooler global climate and the creation of huge glaciers, more than a mile thick, that covered two large areas of land in what is now Canada. The enormous amount of water required to form the world's glaciers lowered the sea level by 300 feet, exposing an immense, 1,000-mile-wide plain between Siberia and Alaska known as Beringia (See map. This land is now covered by water of the Bering Sea.) This tundra-like plain, especially along the coast, teemed with animal and plant life, while the ocean provided abundant marine life.

Scientists and scholars think that early people hunting game and gathering plants for food while traversing Beringia crossed to North America from Asia, thus entering a new continent unaware. Virginia Indians today—mostly unconcerned by the theories of scientists—believe that their origin goes back into the mist of time and that they have always been here.

The first recognized artifact of Paleoindian culture was discovered at Folsom, New Mexico, in 1927, when a distinctive spear point dating to 8500 BC was found lodged between the ribs of a type of bison that had been extinct since the end of the last ice age. Five years later, near

Asians explored Beringia, an exposed fertile land mass in the Bering Sea, during the Pleistocene Age. They traveled either along the coast of present-day Canada or along a corridor between glaciers to the Great Plains. Shaded areas indicate land then above sea level. The large white masses are the Cordilleran and Laurentide ice sheets, over two miles thick in places. (Frank H. McClung Museum, The University of Tennessee)

Clovis, New Mexico, a woolly mammoth kill and associated stone tools dating to 9200 BC were uncovered. The hallmark of the Clovis culture is the bifacially flaked, lance-shaped fluted point. Although Clovis points are found across the continent, an especially large number of them have been retrieved in Virginia.

What has opened a dispute among scientists about the earliest entry of people into the Americas is the discovery of artifacts at several archaeological sites in North and South America. These artifacts, coupled with scientists' conclusions drawn from new DNA and linguistic studies, hint at a much earlier date of 25,000 to 30,000 BC for the earliest arrival of people into the Western Hemisphere. In particular, discussion surrounds pre-Clovis dates and tools recovered at a number of sites, including the Cactus Hill Site in southern Virginia. Here, a small group of people lived on top of a sandy hill overlooking the Nottoway River. One piece of white pine found at Cactus Hill yielded a radiocarbon date of almost 15,000 BC. Associated with the pine are stone flake blades and the cores from which they were struck.

If people lived in Virginia by 15,000 BC, as it now appears, then scientists need to reconsider how people might have entered the Western

Cores (top row) and blade flakes (bottom row) from the pre-Clovis level at the Cactus Hill Site. (Nottoway River Survey)

Hemisphere. The previously accepted theory, as explained above, held that humans entered North America from Asia, walking across Beringia. They then moved south toward the Great Plains, passing through an "ice-free" corridor between the vast Cordilleran and Laurentide glaciers. The corridor was necessary because glaciers flowing down from the mountains into the sea blocked a clear path south by land along the Pacific coast. However, according to geologists, the interglacial corridor opened between 12,500 and 11,500 BC, obviously later than the evidence for human activity at Cactus Hill. As a result, many archaeologists, scientists, and other scholars now speculate that people hunting marine and land mammals moved by boats along the coast of Beringia and on down the coasts of present-day Canada, the United States, and Central America into South America. Descendents of these people then migrated into the heartland of North and South America.

A few archaeologists have turned to Europe and Australia for another hypothesis. They suggest that people living on the Iberian Peninsula (present-day Spain and Portugal) or in Australia used boats to travel to the Western Hemisphere by passing along the edge of ice sheets extending into the North Atlantic and the South Pacific oceans. These people also would have been adapted to fishing and hunting sea mammals.

Regardless of how people arrived in the Americas, from 15,000 BC until approximately 8000 BC, the climate and environment of the two continents differed dramatically from what they are now. The effects of the glaciers made for long, hard winters and short, cool summers. In the Appalachian region, the mountain slopes were bare and tundra-like. People in the Shenandoah Valley and northern Virginia lived among grasslands; open forests of conifers such as pine, fir, spruce, and hemlock; and occasional islands of deciduous trees. Slightly warmer weather south of present-day Richmond encouraged the growth of more deciduous trees such as birch, beech, and oak.

The first people lived in groups anthropologists call *bands,* which can be likened to an extended family. They camped along streams that flowed through the tundra-like grasslands and the open spruce, pine,

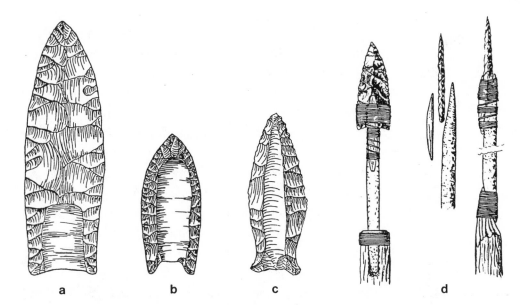

a   b   c   d

and fir forests covering most of Virginia at that time. Because of the harsh climate, these bands also moved seasonally within a set territory to hunt and forage.

As they had for thousands of years, bands roamed the land, hunting herd animals and gathering a variety of plants. Many scientists call the people of this period Big Game Hunters, but the term is not entirely accurate. The western bands are known to have stalked bison and the now-extinct mammoth and mastodon. But caribou were more common in the northeast, and in Virginia deer, elk, bear, and moose were plentiful. Scientists have no proof that Virginia Paleoindians hunted big game, though it was available there. In Saltville, in Southwest Virginia, geologists have found fossils of mastodon, ground sloth, mammoth, and extant (but not in Virginia today) musk ox, caribou, moose, and bison.

Salt licks, lakes, and rivers attracted animals large and small, and the people followed the game. To bring down the animals, the hunters needed to develop the proper tools. Their inventions signaled the new technology of the Clovis period. The Thunderbird Paleoindian Site, near a jasper quarry in today's northern Shenandoah Valley, was a favored gathering place for Clovis toolmaking in the region. People used it for 2,000 years, leaving behind stone artifacts in a series of quarry sites and base camps established for tool manufacturing and hunting. Other stone tools found at Thunderbird and associated with Clovis points include unifacially flaked scrapers, gravers, perforators, wedges, and bi-

Stylistic changes in Paleoindian fluted points allow scientists to date the era and region in which they were made: a. Clovis, 10,000–9000, Rocky Mountains to the Atlantic coast; b. Folsom, 9000–8000 BC, western plain; c. Cumberland, 9000–8000 BC, Ohio and Tennessee river drainages; d. hafting technique and bone foreshaft for attaching fluted point to a spear or knife handle. (Copyright 1976 by the American Association for the Advancement of Science)

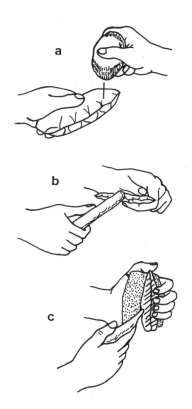

Projectile point flaking required great skill:
a. use of a hammer-stone prepared the general outline of the point;
b. precise blows with a bone hammer gave the point its shape;
c. careful detailed pressure flaking completed the task by refining the point's edge.

facial and unifacial knives. Evidence uncovered so far in Virginia suggests that these tools were used to spear game, cut up meat, scrape and cut hides, and split and carve the bone of deer, bison, and rabbit. Caribou, elk, moose, and mastodon also may have been hunted. Thunderbird marks a region where social cooperation and the sharing of ideas and innovations ensured survival. Today, the area of the Thunderbird Site Complex forms one of the most significant archaeological zones in eastern North America, stratigraphically linking cultures from the Paleoindian through the Early Archaic eras.

Scientists studying Thunderbird and other related sites and similar bands of people have developed a picture of the way these early people lived. For instance, because written records did not exist, the first people relied on storytelling to bind one generation to the next. The storytellers within each band were revered because of the great knowledge they possessed. Listening to the storytellers speak with great eloquence and expression, and with the aid of counters and hieroglyphics, the people learned their history by heart. The stories were "factual" records of the life of their culture; mythical tales conveyed moral truths. A band's oral history served a great purpose, teaching its members how to survive and uphold beliefs and traditions. Virginia Indians, today, continue the storytelling tradition.

Early Archaic Period, 8000–6000 BC

The term archaic, meaning old, signals a series of new adaptations by the early Indians that occurred between 8000 and 1200 BC. During the time of the Paleoindians, the ocean was three hundred feet lower than it is today. The Chesapeake Bay was just a narrow river. As the cold, moist climate of the Pleistocene Age changed to a warmer, drier one, the warming winds melted the glaciers hundreds of miles to the north and warmed the ocean water. The sea level rose, spreading water across the Coastal Plain of Virginia. This change created the bay and covered or eroded most of the places where the early hunters and dispersed foragers lived. Open grassland gave way to woods of pine and oak. As the fauna changed, the mastodon, the last of the large Pleistocene animals on the scene, became extinct, and the number of bison dwindled. People hunted widely abundant elk, deer, and bear. And, most likely,

WHAT WERE THEY LIKE?

The Lifestyles and Customs of the PALEOINDIAN PEOPLE

Throughout the book, simple scenarios such as the one that follows are presented to show what life was like during each period of the first people. Based on scanty archaeological findings and analogy, the lifestyle of Paleoindian band members could be described like this:

Together with six men, the young hunter waded across the river to the jasper quarry. Along a geological fault, they searched for the yellow stone that made the best tools. The men dug at the earth with their tools, exposing the jasper and then breaking it off. Lugging the chunks to the riverbank, they shaped them into pieces that could easily be carried across the river to camp.

The hunters adeptly flaked the stone into knives for cutting, drills for piercing, gravers for incising, scrapers for cleaning hides and shaving wood, and wedges for splitting wood or bone. The yellow jasper flaked easily and uniformly as they hammered the stone with river rocks. Two highly skilled hunters in the band made the lance-shaped spear points, which were channeled and then easily fitted and attached to a wooden spear, replacing the old, worn points. They would use these spears for thrusting and throwing into game.

In a few days, after the tools were ready, the six men left the base camp to hunt. They traveled to the nearby marshes and bogs, which attracted large game. Hiding in the underbrush, they waited for three moose to stop for a drink of water before charging for the kill. Then they skinned and quartered the animals with their heavy chopping and cutting tools. After the hunters divided the portions among themselves for their families, the women moved the pieces from the marsh and stripped the carcasses of bone and meat.

The band that sat around the fire that night was made up of four families. Each member of the band had a special task. The men made tools, chopped down saplings for shelter, and hunted animals. The women raised the children, gathered plants, made clothing, and used the saplings and animal hides to build shelters. Everyone shared his and her talents with the group.

Several weeks after the hunt, the men returned to the quarry and gathered materials for their depleted tool supply. As the weather turned and winter settled in the valley, three other bands arrived at the camp. They would remain there until the spring, when all the households would disperse to find fresh hunting ground. The young hunter looked forward to the evening gathering, when the storyteller would spin his tales. Through these stories, the young and old alike learned by heart the legends of creation and how to survive day by day. The stories told them how they were connected to the spirits of the mountains, rivers, trees, rocks, wind, and sun. At the gathering, the people would contact the spirits in offerings, prayers, and trances to appease good spirits and drive away bad ones.

as the vegetation became profuse, they gathered more plant foods, such as fruit and nuts.

The people of the Archaic period began to vary the size and shape of their lithic (stone) tools. Stone spear points, knives, scrapers, engravers, and drills were still used; however, the hunter-gatherers fashioned them differently, with side or corner notches. Notching tells us how the points were attached to smaller spears that were commonly thrown, like a javelin.

In their hunting, the Early Archaic people prized animal skins, especially deer, for their many uses. Thongs, clothing, blankets, containers, and shelter coverings were made from various skins. At camp, the women would prepare them by first removing all remaining flesh and fat with a hafted stone scraper. Next, they stretched and dried the pelt. Sometimes it was soaked in water and again scraped to remove all the hair. To soften the pelt, the women rubbed oak bark or deer brains into the skin. To complete the softening and waterproofing of the pelt, they then pounded and stretched it over a smoking fire.

The Indians in Early Archaic times made widespread use of rockshelters to protect themselves from the weather, leaving behind many well-preserved sites. Rockshelters of sandstone and limestone are common in the mountains of Virginia. The caves frequently formed when ground water dissolved the limestone bedrock. Luckily for archaeologists, the shelters serve as time capsules of various cultures. Within them, the limestone neutralizes the acidity of the soil and preserves even the smallest bone and shell objects, which often would be dissolved in an open site.

At Daugherty's Cave in Russell County, archaeologists searched through 10 layers of soil to a depth of nine feet. Indians first lived in

Projectile points commonly crafted by peoples of the Early Archaic period (left to right: Palmer, Fort Nottoway, Kirk Stemmed, LeCroy).

this large rockshelter 9,800 years ago. They continued to use it until the 1600s. Archaeologists uncovered a wide variety of stone and bone tools scattered around fire-blackened stone hearths and smudge pits. The bone and shell remains from the rockshelter included a long list of mammals, birds, fish, reptiles, amphibians, mussels, and aquatic snails. Various charred nut shells, seeds, and corn were also found. These discoveries provided scientists with a detailed picture of what the people ate and what the environment may have been like for over 9,000 years. Findings suggest the Indians probably spent their days preparing food, knapping stone tools, smoke curing animal hides, sewing leather into clothes and bags, and repairing tools and weapons.

In general, the Early Archaic population grew, nurtured by a more-inviting environment. Archaeological sites from this period are far more common and larger than those from the Ice Age. Paleoindian people lived in small groups, moving frequently within territories to hunt and forage. Families in the Archaic times lived in larger bands and remained mobile, but within a more limited fertile area.

Early hunters, around 6500 BC, roamed in small bands and set up camps along rivers and hilltops near sources of food, transportation, and raw materials for tools and supplies. (Illustration by Thomas Whyte, Frank H. McClung Museum, The University of Tennessee)

Dispersed Foragers

*My ancestors believed that Mother Earth was our great provider
as the Great Spirit intended her to be. She provides us with beauty
in all things. She provides us with food, shelter, clothing, and tools.
Our ancestors handed down through each generation the belief in
the importance of living in peace and harmony with Mother Earth
to provide the balance needed in the environment.*
—Shirley Custalow McGowan, Little Dove,
    Mattaponi Indian Tribe

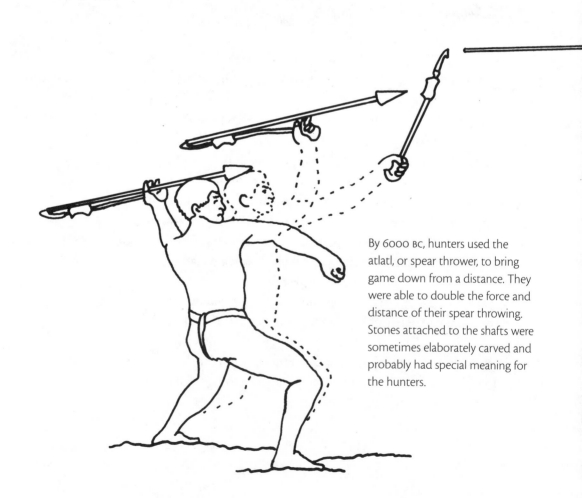

By 6000 BC, hunters used the
atlatl, or spear thrower, to bring
game down from a distance. They
were able to double the force and
distance of their spear throwing.
Stones attached to the shafts were
sometimes elaborately carved and
probably had special meaning for
the hunters.

Middle Archaic Period, 6000–2500 BC

By this time, the Indians of Virginia had adjusted well to the Eastern woodland. They now lived in a climate that had shifted from long winters and short summers and tended toward seasons much like those of today. Increased rains caused much flooding of rivers, which deposited rich topsoil on the surrounding plains. The people became masters of the deciduous forests of oak and chestnut. They moved about easily, hunting and gathering according to the seasons. Their knowledge of how best to use the physical setting shifted with the changing environment and gradually became more sophisticated and effective.

To perform their tasks effectively, the Middle Archaic people enlarged their tool kits, becoming skilled at new challenges. The Native American array of tools now included an innovation called an "atlatl," a spear thrower that added length and power to the hunter's arm. Archae-ologists have found parts of spear throwers—the hooks and stones—at sites as old as 6000 BC. The hooks, made from bone or antler, held the butt end of the spear. The polished stones were attached below the hook. The purpose of the atlatl stone is uncertain. It may have balanced and steadied the spear as the hunter followed through on his throw. The stones uncovered in excavations are generally well made from beautiful types of stone and vary in shape over the years. As works of art, they probably had special meaning to the hunter. Other tools archaeologists commonly find in gathering societies such as this one are mortars and pestles. These tools were used to crush nuts and seeds, to prepare foods so they could be digested easily.

The people of the Eastern forest produced an early form of ax around 5000 BC by notching and chipping it entirely from tough resilient stone, such as basalt and quartzite. By contrast, in 3000 BC, they flaked, pecked, and then smoothed the stone to make grooved axes. With axes, the Middle Archaic people could more easily cut wood to build houses and make fires. The forest clearings that resulted altered the environment in a radical way. Deer, bear, turkey, and other animals came to the clearings to browse on the tender leaves and shoots of low-lying shrubs

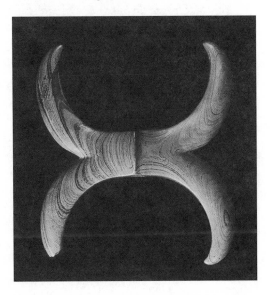

This atlatl stone was carefully pecked and polished from beautiful banded slate. (Private collection. Photo courtesy of the College of William and Mary Center for Archaeological Research.)

WHAT WERE THEY LIKE?

The Lifestyles and Customs of the MIDDLE ARCHAIC PEOPLE

Based on scientific findings, a scene from the lives of the Middle Archaic people probably appeared like this:

The elder looked up from the riverbank to see the men returning in the dugout canoe. By their boisterous talk, he knew their trip had been a good one—they had found enough mussels upstream to feed the band for several days. After the lean winter, the spring was a relief and a joy. Soon there would be enough food for them all to eat, with turtles coming out of hibernation and migrating geese and ducks returning. Tender green plants were sprouting and filling out. The women would make flour from the starchy roots.

Shouts of the women and children announced their return to camp. They brought young shoots, snails, grubs, and other delicacies from their foraging. Everyone laughed, anticipating how good the rabbit caught in one of the traps would taste. If the men were successful in their hunt, they would eat until they became full and drowsy.

The band enjoyed its leisure. For four or five hours a day, the people gathered, hunted, and made the tools they needed to survive. The rest of the time, they told stories, worshipped, and played.

A month later, in late spring, the elder helped break camp. The food supplies were gone, and now each of the households headed alone into the Great Valley to camp along the stream and rivers, where food would be more plentiful. Throughout the summer, the elder's household moved from one location to another in search of food. The women combed the area, foraging for strawberries, blackberries, raspberries, and grapes. Meanwhile, the men used the camp as a staging area and made periodic treks to the mountains to hunt wild turkey and deer.

The previous fall, the elder's household had camped on the mountain top at the big meadow. The hunting that season had been very good, and the women had found a great harvest of acorns, walnuts, and hickory nuts. The women had gathered and ground them into meal. With those provisions, the band had stored enough food to last until the spring. The elder hoped the approaching fall and winter would be as generous.

With the bitter cold weather, the household moved back toward the river. The river and its bottomlands were always the most dependable larder, for even in the dead of winter, they could dig turtles out of the frozen mud and hunt deer and other mammals that came to the river for water.

The elder was dismayed; while his household had brought ample stores of food to eat, the other households joining the winter base camp had not. In sharing, there would be little for each. He hoped he would not have to resort to stewing lichens or the bark of the slippery elm tree, two thoroughly distasteful dishes. Still, the elder anticipated the talk fests, dances, singing, and visiting that would take place at this time. As winter progressed, the men left on hunting trips for days at a time. The elder shivered and pulled his skin robe tightly to himself and looked forward to the warmth and abundance of spring.

An important tool in the Eastern forest, the ax changed shape over time: (top) an early ax, notched and chipped from stone, 5000 BC; (middle) grooved ax, 3000 BC; and (bottom) celt, AD 1500, flaked, pecked, then smoothed with sand.

and to eat berries and nuts. With the game coming to them, the Indians found their hunting much easier. Clearing an area dense with trees also encouraged the growth of plants and trees that were beneficial to the Indians, such as berry bushes and fruit and nut trees. Archaeologists point to this practice as an early example of people making changes to the environment that brought them direct benefits.

By now, numerous types of spear points were used throughout the

Projectile Points of Virginia

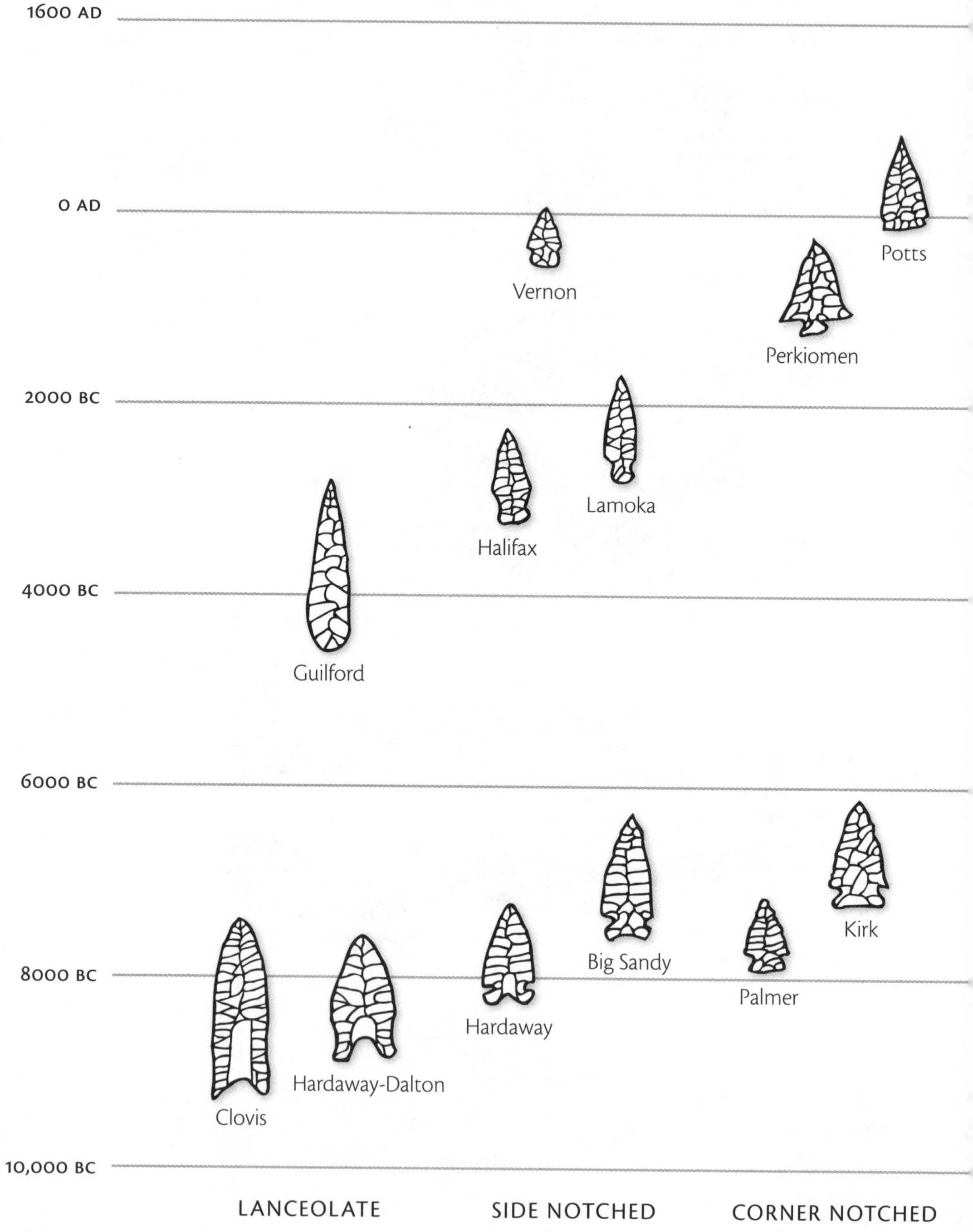

1600 AD

0 AD

Vernon

Potts

Perkiomen

2000 BC

Lamoka

Halifax

Guilford

4000 BC

6000 BC

Big Sandy

Kirk

8000 BC

Hardaway

Palmer

Clovis

Hardaway-Dalton

10,000 BC

LANCEOLATE   SIDE NOTCHED   CORNER NOTCHED

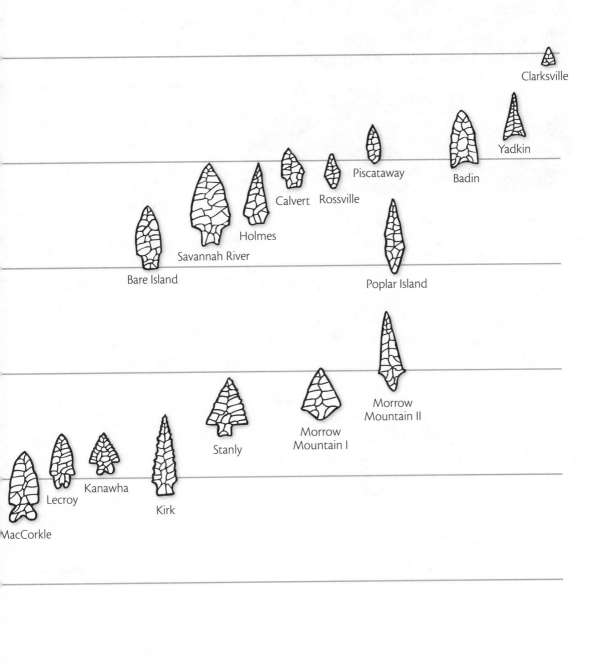

Clarksville

Yadkin

Badin

Piscataway

Calvert Rossville

Holmes

Savannah River

Bare Island

Poplar Island

Morrow
Mountain II

Stanly

Morrow
Mountain I

Kanawha

Lecroy

Kirk

MacCorkle

BIFURCATE   SQUARE   TAPERING   TRIANGULAR

Native American women used pestles (stones for grinding and pounding), and mortars (flat stones hollowed out from use), to crush nuts and seeds in preparing flour and other foods that could be easily digested.

eastern United States. Many of them are found in Virginia. Archaeologists use point styles in vogue at a particular time to determine the period in which people lived at a site.

Since all projectile points have similar tips, archaeologists look carefully at their bases to identify types. The shape of the base reflects how the point was hafted (or attached), onto the spear, knife, or arrow. Bases were lance shaped, side notched, corner notched, bifurcated, squared, tapered, or triangulated. Some points were flaked to create toothlike serrated edges, perhaps for cutting fibrous vegetables and meat. If a spear point broke or became dull and needed to be resharpened by pressure flaking, the shape of the blade changed drastically. In this situation, the base, the part covered with the sinew and glue of the hafting, was not altered.

Sedentary Foragers

Thoughts are like arrows. Once released, they strike their mark.
Guard them well, or one day you may be your own victim.
—Old Indian axiom, Chickahominy Indian Tribe

Late Archaic Period, 2500–1200 BC

The Indians in Virginia now totaled perhaps tens of thousands. Their large numbers caused them to intensify their hunting and gathering practices. Concentrations of bands settled along the rich floodplain, which some researchers describe as the "supermarket of the prehistoric world." With its new forests and profuse plant and animal life, the floodplain offered the Late Archaic people the widest possible variety of foods. During this period, they added many different types of seeds, shoots, tender leaves, roots, and berries to their diet.

Part of the early Indian tool kit: stone knives hafted to wooden handles. The Indians carried the knives in sheaths sewn from animal skins, such as deer.

Settlement around 1500 BC: bands formed by two or three families produced a lifestyle that afforded considerable leisure after basic survival needs were met. (Illustration by Thomas Whyte, Frank H. McClung Museum, The University of Tennessee)

As more and more groups sought the abundant environment along the rivers, they merged through bonds of marriage and trade to form small settlements, called hamlets. Each hamlet, of from 25 to 50 people, began to take on a simple tribal identity. Elders guided the group, along with members whose talents made them leaders in specific tasks. This structure was unlike earlier bands in which each member held equal standing.

By analogy, archaeologists also assume the people practiced animism, believing that the forces of nature and its elements held superhuman abilities. Through their prayers, stories, and legends, they felt guided through life. Their customs marked the passages of their lives from childhood to adulthood; their rituals marked the cycles of time. They shared a common vision of the universe.

Archaeologists have uncovered at riverside sites large hearths of fire-cracked rock, proof that the Late Archaic people cooked large amounts of food to eat and perhaps to store. By this time, people were learning to nurture native plant species, including sunflowers, sumpweed, maygrass, lambs quarter, smartweed, and perhaps giant ragweed or amaranth. By 2500 BC, people in the eastern United States also started to raise varieties of gourds and squash, which were brought from Mexico, where they were first developed. These were often used as containers for storing food. Findings show they stored extra foodstuffs—smoked fish, deer meat, and nuts—for the lean winter and spring months in pits dug in or near their homes. These pits were similar in function to root cellars, which early colonists built under the floors of their houses.

In the Coastal Plain, the people harvested large numbers of saltwater oysters. Especially in the early spring, before plants came up, oysters were a rich food source. The discarded shells formed thick middens, or refuse heaps, piled up along with other household debris. Shell middens from the Late Archaic period and later sites are common along the coast of Virginia. Earlier sites are rare, however. They became submerged when the sea level rose and the coastline started to change around 10,000 BC.

In their quest for food and raw materials, the Indians ventured into the mountains of western Virginia in greater numbers and more often than before. On high mountain meadows and in saddles, gaps, and hollows, they searched for stones of rhyolite and quartzite to make their tools, hunted game, and gathered nuts and berries in season.

Soapstone, commonly found along the eastern foothills of the Blue Ridge from Fairfax to Floyd County, was one of the most sought-after materials around 2000 BC. A type of soft rock that carved easily and did not break when heated, it made excellent cooking pots. With the innovation of soapstone vessels, the Indians were able to cook much more efficiently. The people quarried large mushroom-shaped pieces of soapstone from outcroppings. With stone and bone tools, they hollowed out

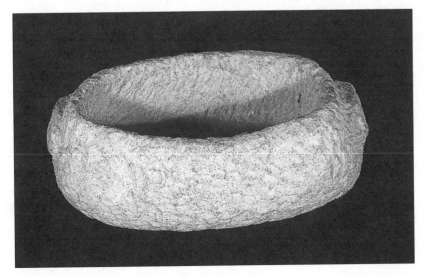

Early Indians, between 2500 and 1200 BC, discovered that easily shaped soapstone made excellent bowls. Cooking became much more efficient with this innovation. (John W. Tisdale Collection)

bowls. Archaeologists have found fragments of soapstone vessels across Virginia, sometimes hundreds of miles from the quarry. When people started making heavy soapstone cooking vessels, they were probably more settled, as the vessels were too heavy to move often. Finding these vessels in different regions of Virginia confirms that people living in the mountains and along the coast engaged in widespread trading.

In excavations of Late Archaic sites, archaeologists have found the remains of dogs, the Indians' only domesticated animal. Man's best friend for thousands of years, the dog served as a companion, a source of food, and as a scavenger around the hamlet.

As pottery became widespread after 1200 BC, Native American women discovered a means of readily making a wide variety of containers for carrying, cooking, and storage. This vessel, dating to AD 1600, has sand-tempered clay and is surface treated with a knotted-net fabric.

Early Woodland Period, 1200–500 BC

The Woodland period refers to the more sedentary cultures that lived in the extensive woodlands of the eastern United States. The period is divided into three sections, beginning in 1200 BC and ending with the arrival of the European settlers.

A major innovation occurred in the Early Woodland period about 1200 BC, when the people began making fired-clay cooking and storage vessels. Archaeologists believe this technology was introduced to Virginia from the people along the coast of South Carolina and Georgia. The earliest pottery in North America was made there beginning about 2500 BC. The shape and size of the first pottery in Virginia was patterned after that of soapstone vessels. Clay pots quickly proved to be more versatile and practical than soapstone.

Archaeologists think the women of the tribe probably fashioned the pottery. People dug good

clay from along a river-bank or a bluff. The women carefully prepared the clay by adding water and temper (crushed rock or shell) to reduce shrinking and cracking during drying and firing. They did not use a pottery wheel; all pieces were hand built. They added clay in pieces to flat bottoms and molded the sides to form low vessels. Soon they learned that they could build up the sides of a vessel higher, faster, and more uniformly by adding coils of clay, one on top of the other. The women pinched the coils of a vessel together and shaped the interior by scraping the walls. The exterior of the vessel was shaped with a paddle wrapped with cord, fabric, or net. The patterns left by the paddling provide archaeologists with rare examples of textiles that seldom survive hundreds of years of burial in the earth. Finally, the vessel was thoroughly air dried and placed in an open fire to bake. When cool, the product was a hard and durable container. The conical bottom of the vessel made it tilt to one side. Such a base held advantages over a flat-bottomed one—it was strong, heated the pot's contents quickly, and could be easily propped up on burning logs by three rocks.

Though pottery vessels were fragile and easily broken, they could be replaced quickly. Superior cooking pots, they also provided drier storage than earlier fiber or skin vessels did. Archaeologists have recorded the changes over time in the temper, size, shape, surface treatment, and decoration of pottery from 1200 BC to the present. This wealth of pottery information provides archaeologists with ways to help date sites and to describe Indian groups and interpret their interaction and movement.

Small platform pipe carved and polished from soft stone illustrates the attention to shape and design that Middle Woodland people lavished on pipes.

Middle Woodland Period, 500 BC–AD 900

Populations grew in Virginia to the point that diverse tribes now lived in scattered settled hamlets clustered along major rivers that wound through the mountain valleys and down through the Piedmont and the Coastal Plain.

One example of this great diversity can be found in the Stone Mound Burial culture in the northern Shenandoah Valley. The Stone Mound Burial people, dating from 400 BC to AD 200, placed hundreds of low stone mounds in clusters on ancient blufflike river terraces overlooking the floodplain. They buried only a few people in each mound.

Sometimes they placed rare and sacred objects made from exotic materials in their graves. These objects included tubular and platform pipes, copper beads, hematite cones, basalt celts, spear-throwing stones, and caches of projectile points. The people placed the objects within the mound for the deceased to use on their afterlife journeys. The few graves within each mound, the few clusters of mounds, and the

Small villages, or hamlets, AD 350, formed the beginnings of ranked societies. Members contributed to the whole through assigned tasks—raising crops, processing animal hides, making pottery and tools, and hunting. (Illustration by Thomas Whyte, Frank H. McClung Museum, The University of Tennessee)

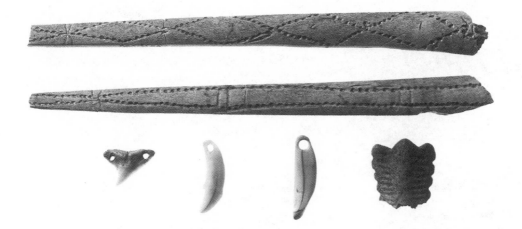

special objects suggest that the Stone Mound Burial people gave only higher-ranking people this preferential treatment.

Elaborately incised bone hairpin and perforated canine and shark's teeth used as ornaments dating to the Middle Woodland period.

The Stone Mound Burial culture is closely related to the Adena culture identified in the Ohio Valley region. This highly developed culture constructed large earthen mounds over the graves of their honored people. They made many elaborate tools and ornaments from high-grade chert and copper and placed them with the dead.

About 2,000 years ago, a domesticated plant was brought into the eastern United States from Mexico, a plant that ushered in many changes. Corn, or maize, by that time had been nurtured from a small, wild stubby nub of a plant to one with large ears, producing long rows of kernels. Archaeologists have found different kinds of charred corn remains, which suggests that corn was hardy and adapted easily to the environment. The Middle Woodland people stopped nurturing other seeds and planted corn. Scientists surmise that the slow introduction of corn helped increase the population during the end of the Middle Woodland era in the eastern United States and that the religious ceremonies surrounding the planting and harvesting of corn may have triggered the elaborately ranked societies that followed.

The people retired their spears and now used the bow and arrow, fletched with turkey feathers, as a new hunting weapon. Evidence for this change is seen in smaller projectile points, particularly the triangular shapes, which were attached with sinew and glue (made from animal hooves) to the ends of the arrow shafts. Further advances came as the people redesigned the grooved ax and used what is called a celt. With an ax, the people could do coarse work; with the celt, they refined their technique. Curved and polished, the ungrooved celt enabled them

Middle Woodland people used the celt, an important technological advance that enabled them to become much more efficient at woodworking.

to work wood quickly and accurately. The hollowed-out socket in the wooden handle did two things—at the same time it securely held the celt's head, it also ensured easy removal for resharpening. In trade, the Indians obtained special materials used for their sacred objects. Everywhere the tribal traders cast networks, they spread their culture's ideas, traditions, and beliefs. These ideas could differ widely from tribe to tribe. They also shared ideas of social organization, views of the natural world, and information about farming.

A number of developments point to the beginnings of ranked cultures. As the Middle Woodland people promoted specialized crafts and increased their trade, status became more valued within a tribe. With these changes, small villages moved toward ranked, complex organizations, where levels of status were bestowed on individuals and families.

Farmers

In former times, the opening of a clay mine was a great feast day
for the Pamunkey. The whole tribe, men, women, and children,
were present, and each family took home a share of the clay.
—Chief Terrill Bradby, Pamunkey Indian Tribe,
   at the turn of the 20th century

Late Woodland Period, AD 900–1600

People throughout the eastern United States lived in thousands of large
villages. Hundreds, if not thousands, of people resided in each village,
which was organized around a complex economic, social, and political structure. The people depended on intensive gardening for most of
their food. Before the Middle Woodland era, tribes scattered throughout Virginia differed little. By Middle to Late Woodland, however,
they developed strong identities as each adapted to its social setting. In
Southwest Virginia, the transplanted Mississippian and local cultures
thrived; in the Shenandoah Valley, the Earthen Mound Burial culture
grew; and to the east, the Coastal Plain Indians prospered.

No longer nomadic, these people lived in societies that answered
their short- and long-term needs. Village life broadened the social
sphere, wealth, and security of the residents. It also required that they
give up time to work in the fields and build homes for a growing community. The resulting social structure demanded more coordination of
functions from the tribal leader. In chiefdoms, for example, the leaders
collected goods in tribute and then politically redistributed them according to need. While the system probably reduced the influence of
some people, it encouraged the creative efforts of others. Artistic and
ceremonial life flowered. Scientists can only guess to what heights the
culture could have gone if the coming of the European settlers had not
disrupted it.

The Late Woodland people achieved a richness of culture that was unmatched to date. They created a wide range of pottery forms and ceremonial and symbolic objects of stone, copper, and shell. Symbolic designs reflected an extensive mythology and belief system that included natural and supernatural figures. Sophisticated burial customs reflected the people's view of the world as a timeless cycle, as a continuous, unchanging procession of death and rebirth.

Village construction patterns in the Eastern United States became more complex; house building more substantial. In hamlets, the homes were scattered between the fields. In villages, various sizes of homes were placed in rows around a plaza, with perhaps a council house or temple elevated on a nearby mound. A palisade may have surrounded the entire village.

In farming, beans arrived from the southwestern North American continent about AD 1000 to join corn and squash as the three major crops. Tobacco came by way of Mexico. To plant their crops, the women and elderly men of the village used digging sticks to plant seeds in little hills of earth spaced three feet apart. Archaeologists believe the vegetables were often planted together, with the squash covering the ground and the beans climbing up the corn stalks, which were planted in the middle. To clear acres of ground and create fields for planting,

Two styles of Late Woodland homes: oval-shaped houses were shared by up to 10 family members. Smaller family groups lived in domed houses. Sections of matting could be removed for ventilation. (Michele Moldenhauer, Archeological Society of Virginia)

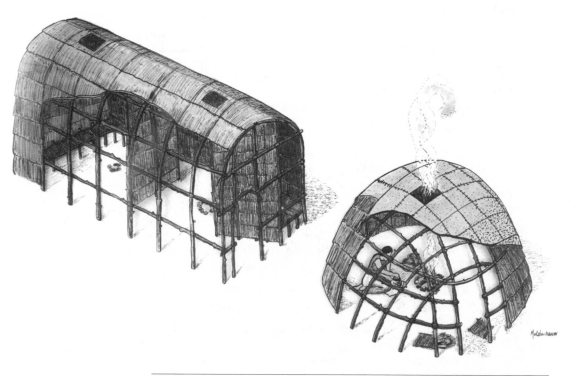

the Woodland Indians relied heavily on the slash-and-burn method. To get the highest yield from their plantings, they rotated use of fields and harvested 5 to 20 bushels of food per acre.

Some archaeologists use the concept of "cultural and natural areas" to explain further how the distinct cultures of the era came about. According to their theory, the environment in which a society settled presented a particular setting, and the people made choices within that setting. Without external forces, a culture was inclined to change slowly once it adjusted to a setting. It was also inclined to spread over an entire area before expanding to a different environment. In Virginia, the Coastal Plain, Piedmont, and mountain regions created distinct natural areas. Cultures spread along the major rivers and streams that flowed within and between each region. Because pieces of the information puzzle are missing, much of the group variation across Virginia has not been fully described nor individual cultures defined. However, we know these things about a few of the more prominent populations:

Southwest Virginia

Local Culture

The mountains and valleys of Southwest Virginia formed a crossroads of Native American culture. Mississippian people entered the region along the Tennessee River system. Ohio Valley groups came in by way of the New River (one of the oldest rivers in the world). And Piedmont cultures advanced up the Roanoke River.

The people of Southwest Virginia formed a tribal culture known for its wide use of limestone, sand, or shell-tempered pottery impressed with cord and net; dome-shaped homes about 20 feet in diameter clustered around a plaza in the center of a palisaded village; and lifestyles based on intensive gardening, supplemented with wild plants and animals.

From the charred remains of plants found in excavations, we know the local people ate corn, beans, squash, gourds, sunflower seeds, persimmons, berries such as grape, and nuts such as acorn, hickory, walnut, and hazelnut. Deer bones also are commonly found, traces of an animal the Indians used completely—meat, bone, fur, sinew, and antler. In hunting, they draped deerskins over their bodies as camouflage to sneak up on the game.

The people depended on other animals for food, too, including turkeys, Eastern cottontail rabbits, raccoons, gray squirrels, black bears, passenger pigeons, turtles, and fish. They fashioned ornamental beads from turkey bones, which, along with the feathers, were used to make headdresses and cloaks.

Recently, archaeologists discovered symbolic figures, or glyphs, in a limestone cave, which the local people drew with their fingers on a thin veneer of soft mud over a rock face. Various curved and rectangular designs compose the figures. What these meant to the Indians, scientists can only guess. Radiocarbon dates of about AD 1000 were obtained from charred fragments of sticks found on the cave floor below the glyphs. Native American mud glyphs are extremely rare and fragile. Because they are not widely recognized, people unaware of what they have discovered can easily destroy them.

The people also made pictographs, or paintings, of red ocher (iron oxide pigment) on the rock faces of mountains. The pictographs show stylized figures of deer, turtles, eagles, arrows, people, and the sun. Pictographs are extremely rare in the eastern United States; Virginia contains only two known examples.

Equally rare are a few vertical-drop burial caves found only in western Virginia, where limestone bedrock occurs. The Indians used these caves, some with vertical drops of more than 100 feet, to inter their dead. Some caves contain the bone remains of more than 100 people. Only one of these unique sites is known to be undisturbed by vandals. In that cave, which is being protected, the tribe buried its men, women, and children.

Drawings of red ocher on a cliff surface reflect symbolic designs the Native Americans used to depict an extensive mythology and belief system. Here, stylized pictures of deer, turtle, people, double-headed bird, arrow, and sun.

People in the 1940s explored this burial cave in Tazewell County, used by a tribe ca. AD 1415 in Southwest Virginia.

Village patterns, pottery, stone tools, and plant and animal remains of the local people are similar over a large region of the mountains and adjacent Piedmont. This evidence tells us that members of neighboring villages traded and came together to celebrate harvests, marriages, and religious ceremonies. They also rallied together for mutual defense in periods of danger.

The first palisaded villages in the region were built around AD 1200. At the Crab Orchard Site in Tazewell County, archaeologists excavated portions of a Late Woodland village in 1971 (before a road was constructed), and again in 1978. Evidence gathered there provided clues as to what the Indians' lives were like. Based on the excavated remains, archaeologists can tell us the following about the village:

The village at the Crab Orchard Site was built around AD 1500. It was 400 feet across and was surrounded with a wall that was replaced three times as the posts decayed. The meaning of the walls remains in question—were they strictly for defense against warring tribes, or did they keep wild animals out? In major villages, the walls may have signaled a more prestigious village.

Within the palisade, the Indians built circular homes in rows around the central plaza and dug many storage and burial pits. They buried hundreds of their people at this site, mainly in the area between the

Artist's rendering of a portion of the Crab Orchard Site showing the large public meeting house, the palisade, and homes. (Illustration by Thomas Whyte)

homes and the palisade. The homes inside the wall were closely spaced and were also rebuilt a number of times. Based on the calculation that 6 to 10 people lived in each of the 50 homes, the population of the village was about 400.

Below the topsoil, small brown spots in the orange subsoil, three to six inches in diameter, show where the people put posts in the ground. The patterns of these spots reveal how they built houses and the palisade. The Indians placed their hearths, now seen in the subsoil as reddish burnt areas, in the middle of their homes and outside, behind their homes. There they roasted food wrapped in leaves, boiled soups, and fired their clay vessels in the coals. Traces of round and oval storage pits and oval burials can be seen as larger brown shapes on the subsoil.

Outside the gate of the village, markings in the soil beyond the palisade show the site's largest structure: the council house, 65 feet long by 30 to 40 feet wide. The floor inside was placed two feet below ground level. A clay bench around the interior gave the people places to sit.

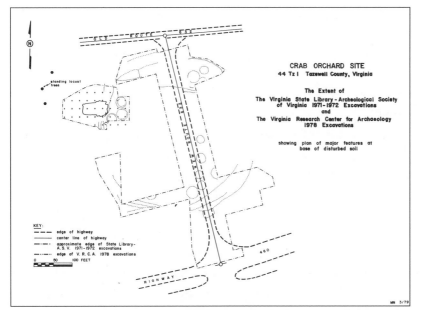

Crab Orchard Site, Taze-well County, holds the archaeological remains of a village of up to 400 people. Archaeological plan drawing shows the house patterns surrounded by palisade lines.

Parallel lines of post-molds and holes of storage and burial pits reveal the edge of a palisaded village.

Directly northeast of this structure are five large storage pits, which the people used to store objects they shared. To the west lay odd-shaped borrow pits. From these, the Indians removed clay to build and maintain the walls of the large structure. Beyond the meeting house were their fields.

The Intrusive Mississippian Culture

During the Late Woodland period in Virginia, Native Americans in other areas of the eastern United States developed a new way of life that archaeologists call "Mississippian." They use this name because some of the first sites of the culture were found along the Mississippi River. A regional phenomenon, the Mississippian culture became widespread throughout the Midwest and southern United States. In Virginia, this culture made its way into the extreme southwestern corner of the state.

The villages of the Mississippian culture were much larger, more complex, and more permanent than other Late Woodland villages. The people cleared and farmed hundreds of acres of river floodplain to support village populations that numbered in the thousands. The more settled and abundant life of the Mississippian culture led to fully developed chiefdoms ruled by chiefs and subchiefs. In a chiefdom, a few highly ranked people at major centers directed the economic, sociopolitical, and religious activities of thousands of people living in a large region. The position of chief became a permanent office; social inequality became a basic rule. Certain items of dress, ornamentation, and food were reserved for one group of people and taboo for others. Goods flowed into the centers and were redistributed by the chiefs to maintain their influence and power. Religion, with its life-cycle rituals and ceremonies, served to support the power of the chief. Ranked individuals sometimes elevated ancestors to supernatural status. The priesthood developed and wielded a position of permanent power within the society.

Indian stone or earthen burial mounds and substructure mounds, similar to the Ely Mound, once numbered in the hundreds in Virginia, until the early 1800s. Years of cultivation, land development, and reforestation have wiped out all but a remaining few.

The people of the Mississippian culture loved games of competition, such as chunkey. In this game of running and precision aiming, they chased chunkey stones in contests against the best players of other villages. (Frank H. McClung Museum, The University of Tennessee)

Tall, distinct, flat-top mounds dominated each of the villages. During the 1800s, most whites believed a "lost race" of Canaanites, the Lost Tribes of Israel, Phoenicians, Greeks, or Vikings built the mounds in the eastern North American continent. Supposedly, this superior race lived there before the Indians did. The whites held that the Indians destroyed the lost race and were incapable of such achievements.

Eventually, archaeologists proved the mounds were built by members of the Mississippian culture who were ancestors of the 19th-century Indians. Lucien Carr, who tested the Ely Mound in Virginia, was one of the first archaeologists to link the Indians with the mound centers in the eastern United States. Further evidence came from the written records of early European explorers and naturalists, who described seeing temples on flat-topped mounds in the villages they visited. The mounds signaled a new and more elaborate way in which the native people symbolized their beliefs.

The Mississippian culture entered Virginia from the southwest along the Tennessee River system. Today, in Lee County near the Tennessee border, a few mounds still exist that may have been built by the ancestors of present-day Cherokee. Located on the edge of the Mississippian influence, these mounds and villages are smaller than the great centers located in the far south.

The Ely Mound, in southwestern Virginia, was studied in the early 1870s. Lucien Carr's archaeological report describes the mound as a "truncated oval . . . about 300 feet in circumference at the base,

Hauntingly beautiful, this shell pendant, or gorget, was similar to others associated with Mississippian culture. This ceremonial object was found in Stafford County, near the Potomac River. Note the "weeping eye," or thunderbolt, motif. (Department of Anthropology, Smithsonian Institution)

and 19 feet in height." Decaying stumps of a series of cedar posts were found on the top of the mound. Archaeologists thought "that the summit of the mound had at one time been occupied by some sort of a building—possibly a rotunda or council chamber." Two unusual artifacts were found that normally were associated with Mississippian culture. A large chunkey stone remained from one of the people's most popular sports, and a shell pendant, with a "weeping eye," or lightning bolt motif, left a trace of their ceremonial garb.

The mound looks the same today as it did in the 1870s. A slight depression at the top of the mound indicates the excavation. An apron of soil fill that extends to the southeast is evidence of a series of steps ascending the side of the mound.

Piedmont and Shenandoah Valley

Earthen Mound Burial Culture

In an area that includes both the Piedmont and the Shenandoah Valley, a culture existed from AD 950 to the time of European contact that

Knife point hafted onto deer antler created a tool for thrusting and cutting.

buried its dead in earthen mounds. Visible monuments on the native landscape, some of these mounds reached a height of at least 20 feet above the surrounding surface. These mounds were distinct in that they served as the final burial place for hundreds, and, in some cases, more than a thousand people. The earliest burials in the mounds were of individuals. Later in time, the bones of many who died were taken and ritually reburied in the mound. Archaeologists call the mounds "accretional mounds," because they were built up over time, with each successive burial ritual adding more to the top of the mound. The mounds today do not look as they did centuries ago. Most of them have been plowed flat and disturbed by flooding.

The mounds were sacred places where ancestors were honored. In 1784 Thomas Jefferson examined one of these mounds near Charlottesville in what many consider to be the earliest scientific archaeological excavation in America. He later wrote that he had watched a group of Indians, in the mid-18th century, walk solemnly to the mound near Charlottesville to conduct a ritual:

> But on whatever occasion they may have been made, they are of considerable notoriety among the Indians: for a party passing, about 30 years ago, through the part of the country where this barrow is, went through the woods directly to it, without any instructions or enquiry, and having staid about it some time, with expressions which were construed to be those of sorrow, they returned to the high road, which they had left about half a dozen miles to pay this visit, and pursued their journey.

The continuation of such rituals is evidence of the importance of these sacred places to the Indians of central Virginia.

The people who built the mounds lived in sedentary villages along the major rivers, typically on and alongside the soils with high agricultural potential. Like their neighbors, they practiced a combination of horticulture and hunting and gathering. Remains of corn and squash have been found in cooking and trash pits in village sites along the James River in the Piedmont. Unfortunately, heavy flooding in the last two centuries, along with destructive plowing methods, have left few villages intact. The outlines of three oval houses were recorded at one village site near Wingina on the James River in Nelson County. Little else is known at this time about how the communities were organized.

The pottery of the area was similar to that of neighboring regions, though it was tempered with quartz and sand. Fabric, net, and cord markings were common, though there were some patterns of decoration common to the Coastal Plain that did not occur in great numbers in the Piedmont.

The people in the Piedmont made most of their stone tools from the locally abundant white quartz; in the Shenandoah Valley and surrounding mountains, the Indians used the better-quality chert and jasper found there. They used the high-quality stones in trade throughout the region. Two rare resources in the region were soapstone and copper.

It is likely that these Late Woodland people in the Piedmont were the ancestors of the Monacan and Manahoac noted by John Smith on his early map of Virginia.

Coastal Plain

Coastal Plain Culture

The Coastal Plain offered a unique environment of saltwater and freshwater rivers, bays, and marshes. People adapted to it by relying on fishing, particularly for the shad and sturgeon that ascended rivers to spawn. From the shallow waters, they gathered shellfish. The Coastal Plain Indians stored large amounts of food to support themselves. Shell middens, great heaps of discarded shells, show they gathered oysters in the late spring, dried them for storage, and disbursed them through the village when there was little else to eat.

By AD 1300, the Coastal Plain tribes had grown to form sedentary villages supported by small short-term hunting and gathering camps. Relying more and more on horticulture, they favored the floodplain

Virginia coastal settlements were very similar to those of Secoton, North Carolina, as depicted by the artist John White. Note (c) the Dancing Circle used to celebrate special times: (f) the raised hut from which young children protected cornfields from the birds. (Engraving by Theodor de Bry, from Thomas Hariot's *A Briefe and True Report of the New Found Land of Virginia* [New York: Dover Publications, 1972])

Reconstruction of an Indian bark-covered house at Jamestown Settlement, Jamestown, Virginia. Dried meats and fish were often stored on horizontal poles or lofts overhead; sleeping benches lined the walls.

and low-lying necklands of rich sandy soil for village sites. The Coastal Plain people built their villages with oval houses close together and perhaps surrounded by a palisade, or with the houses dispersed, separated by fields for gardening.

Through most of the Late Woodland period, the coastal groups formed independent tribal societies. Chiefdoms developed by the 16th century. Hundreds of villages dotted the land. Crowded, competing for territory, and needing to expand their economic systems, the weaker tribes were forced to pay tribute and allegiance to the stronger ones. In return for goods paid in tribute, the member tribes were protected in times of attack and need.

In general, the objects used by the Late Woodland people differed little from those used in the earlier Woodland periods. They worked with the same types of tools and wore ornaments made from wood, bone, and shell. Stone artifacts are commonly found in the inner Coastal Plain near the fall line where rock is ample; however, they are rare along the Atlantic coast simply because little stone existed there. What do remain are traces of pottery. Shell tempered and fabric marked, these pieces were characterized by rectilinear patterns incised into the wet clay below the rim. This type of pottery is found throughout the coastal plain of Virginia, Maryland, and Delaware. Its widespread use suggests a sphere of trade among villages in the entire Chesapeake Bay area.

Burial practices differed according to the status of the person in the tribe. Single burials have been found, as well as ossuaries. Ossuaries are pits in which the bones of many people were placed after their bodies had decomposed. The Coastal Plain people periodically performed ritual burial ceremonies and interred the dead together in a large pit. Before the ceremony, the dead were either kept above ground in mortuary houses or buried and later moved. To the Coastal Plain people, the ossuaries may have stood for the oneness of the community, united in its cycles of life and death in a final common resting place. Burial rites held at these sites may have served to unite dispersed villages within a given subchiefdom.

WHAT WERE THEY LIKE?

The Lifestyles and Customs of the MISSISSIPPIAN PEOPLE

What was daily life like for the Ely Mound people? Based on archaeological findings and interpretation, the following account is a sketch of the lifestyle of the Mississippian culture:

The chief heard the drums beating and knew it was time to join his brother in leading the sacred rites of the new year. Part of the ruling family, his brother served as priest of the temple. The chief, who inherited rule of the village as his mother's eldest son, guided his brothers and sisters and aunts and uncles in leading the villagers. They determined matters of labor, worship, food distribution, training, marriage, and healing.

The chief left his home, surveying the nearby temple that rested atop the large, flat mound overlooking the village. Important social, religious, and secret ceremonies took place there.

He climbed the steps leading up the mound and, with his brother, led the highest-ranking members of the village in a secret service within the temple. Then, they descended the steps in a procession to the plaza, a large open formal area, where the common people had gathered for a ceremony of new year offerings. The chief felt their eagerness to reach the end of the rites and begin the dancing, an event they had looked forward to for months.

As his brother intoned the prayer of new beginnings, the chief surveyed the village. The houses of his priests, caretakers of the ceremonial areas, craft specialists, and warriors were clustered around the plaza. Servants, raided from other villages, were building four new homes. The chief saw the trenches in which the servants would secure posts before filling them in. The walls of the houses were interlaced with slender branches woven horizontally through vertical posts. The masons would daub these with mud and then whitewash them. They would also build a clay fireplace in the center, under a smoke hole in the thatched roof.

The chief caught a glimpse of the homes of the villagers beyond the homes surrounding the plaza. His gaze lingered over the trampled earth serving as their yards, the focus of their family life and chores. Here and there, tools lay idly on the ground, signs of pot making and hide tanning abandoned for the festival.

Later in the day, the chief met with representatives from a neighboring village and agreed on matters of trade. In exchange for ample supplies of corn, beans, and deer meat, the neighboring village offered beautifully decorated pottery and a ceremonial robe resplendent with beadwork of pearls and shells and edged with hawk feathers, which pleased the chief greatly.

Seasons passed; with the coming of the fall and the harvest time, the chief sent a message to the leaders of nearby villages. All were invited to compete in a game similar to lacrosse in the harvested fields. The plaza, where the opening ceremonies for the games would be held, would soon be the site of the year's final chunkey game. The chief's son would compete in it against the priest's son. The chief hoped his son's spear would land closest to the highly polished, circular stone that served as a target.

European Contact, 1607–1800

*Many people either romanticize the American Indian and
believe we live in teepees and ride horses (as did the nomadic
tribes of the Plains) or we are looked down upon. We want to
be known and appreciated for who and what we are.*
—Phyllis B. Hicks, Monacan Indian Nation

Native Peoples along the Coast

When Christopher Columbus debarked on the shores of the Western
Hemisphere, or, more precisely, the West Indies, he believed he had
found a new trade route to Asia. Thinking he had landed in India, he
called the native people "Indians," and so described them to Queen
Isabella upon his return to Spain. The coastal groups in Virginia first
encountered Europeans in 1525. During this early period, the natives

Powhatan women
carried their babies
on cradle boards until
they were old enough
to walk. A layer of red
paint and bear grease
kept the babies' naked
bodies warm in the
winter and cool in the
summer. (Engraving by
Simon Gribelin based on
illustration by Theodor
de Bry, from Robert
Beverley, *The History and
Present State of Virginia*
[rpt. ed., Chapel Hill:
University of North
Carolina Press, 1947])

likely traded with the Europeans to give them fresh water, fruit, and meat. They were alarmed when the Spanish and Portuguese raided their villages and took captives.

The first English colonists in North America arrived in 1584 at Roanoke Island, North Carolina. The next year, a group of these settlers explored southeastern Virginia. The Roanoke colony found it difficult to survive—it ran out of food and supplies. Sir Richard Grenville reportedly burned an Indian village over the alleged taking of a silver cup. An English officer captured and beheaded a chief on the rumor that the Indians planned an attack. In 1590, when the colony's leader, John White, returned from England, he found the settlement deserted. What happened to the "lost colony" remains a mystery to this day.

The first permanent English colony in North American managed to survive at Jamestown in 1607. Although this settlement also ran out of supplies and nearly perished, it grew as increasing numbers of colonists came. By the 1700s, the area known as "Virginia" extended west from the Atlantic Coast to the Mississippi River and north into the Ohio River Valley.

The English under Captain John Smith immediately explored the surrounding country, traveling up the James, York, Rappahannock, and Potomac rivers as far as the fall line (the point at which the rivers drop as they enter the Coastal Plain). They observed and wrote about the many villages and natives they met. One colonist, Henry Spelman, lived with the natives for nearly a year. Smith published an accurate map of the Coastal Plain of Virginia, locating the villages the scouting party discovered. In his writings, Smith noted of the Indians, "The men bestowe their time in fishing, hunting, wars and such manlike exercises. . . . The women and children do the rest of the worke. They make mats, baskets, pots, mortars, pound their corne, make their bread, prepare their victuals, plant their corn, gather their corn, beare al kind of burdens and such like."

About their appearance, he wrote, "[The Powhatans are] generally tall and straight, of a comely proportion, and of a colour browne. . . . Their haire is generally black, but few have any beards. The men weare halfe their heads shaven, the other halfe long. . . . The [women's hair] are cut in many fashions agreeable to their years, but ever some part remaineth long. They are very strong, of an able body and full of agilitie, able to endure to lie in the woods under a tree by the fire, in the worst of winter."

The coastal Indians developed a variety of ways to catch fish: night fires in dugout canoes attracted fish to the surface for spearing; fish weirs created traps from which the fish could not escape; nets also served to harvest big catches. (Engraving by Theodor de Bry, from Thomas Hariot's *A briefe and true report of the new found land of Virginia* [New York: Dover Publications, 1972])

Map of Virginia by Captain John Smith, 1608. Smith and his explorers found hundreds of villages set along the rivers and bays of coastal Virginia.

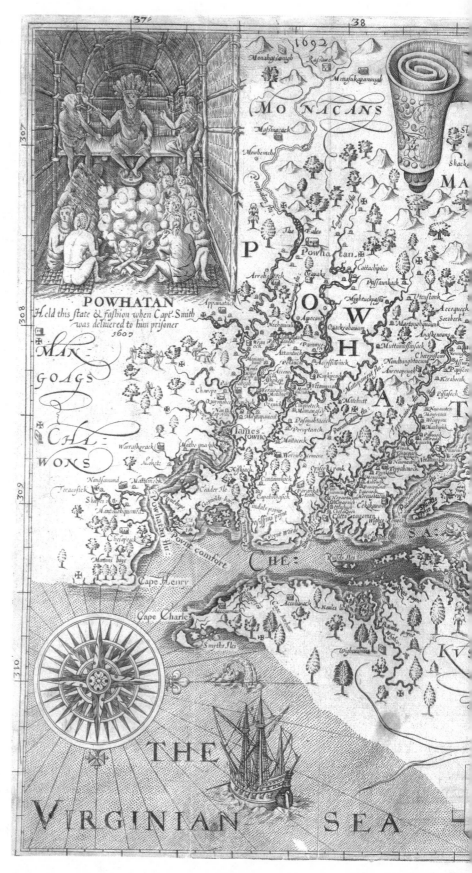

The Indians in coastal Virginia deeply felt the presence of the English settlers. Each culture had differing ideas about the other. When the English saw a large tract of unoccupied land, for example, they assumed it was not in use and therefore available to be claimed. They railed against the Powhatan concept of common property—the idea that open land was a source of food and materials to be shared by all.

The natives regarded land, sky, water, and air as integral parts of the Earth that could not be bought and sold. They saw themselves as part of the Earth, and not vice versa. The Earth, they felt, was precious to their gods and required their protection. The English concept of land ownership caused them concern about the care of wildlife, forests, streams, and the land itself. The settlers wanted more land to expand their settlements and more resources, such as furs and wood, for export to increase their wealth. In this conflict, the Indians at times befriended the settlers, giving them food and teaching them to raise crops, such as corn. At other times, they felt it necessary to repel the colonists who challenged their culture, lifestyle, and their very lives.

The two cultures also clashed over religious beliefs. Religion was an integral part of Powhatan daily life. Through it, every activity was imbued with a higher meaning, be it healing, working, eating, or dancing. The priests practiced a form of medicinal healing that united body and spirit, and the Powhatan sweat lodge was used both for personal and spiritual cleansing. The Powhatans accepted the idea of a Christian deity, because they worshipped many gods. The English, however, felt committed to converting the Indians to Christianity. They did not understand and were angered when the Indians refused to renounce their other gods and worship "the one true God."

Another difference between the cultures was the Powhatans' matrilineal society. Family descent and inheritance passed through the women rather than through men, an idea foreign to the English. Wahunsunacock was the paramount chief, or "Powhatan," of the chiefdom when the colonists first arrived. His title and the name of the chiefdom were one and the same. As Powhatan, Wahunsunacock's rule could pass to his next oldest brother by the same mother, or to the children of his eldest sister, but not to his offspring. Social status in such a society was measured by wealth, obtained through tribute and trade in the form of large amounts of corn, copper, and animal skins.

Most of the coastal Indians (with the exception of the Meherrin and the Nottoway) were Algonquian-speaking people, with a population of approximately 14,000 to 21,000. By 1607 many of the villages of the Algonquian-speaking people were brought under one rule by Wahunsunacock, who formed the Powhatan paramount chiefdom. Wahunsunacock reigned over 32 subchiefdoms in over 150 villages of various sizes, which he controlled through inheritance and power. In war, the districts fought for him; in peace, they paid taxes on their produce. The chief, in return, aided them in times of need.

The colonists offered this description of him: "He is of personage a tall well-proportioned man, with a sower looke, his head somewhat gray, his beard so thinne that it seemeth none at al, his age neare 60; of a very able and hard body to endure any labour." John Smith observed, "The forme of their Common wealth is a monarchical government, one as Emperour ruleth over many kings or governours. Their chiefe ruler is called Powhatan. . . . His inferiour kings whom they cal werowances are tyed to rule by customes, and have power of life and death at their command."

In Powhatan society, men shaved the right side of their heads for precision shooting with bow and arrow. Hair on the left side was often tied and adorned with a feather or tails of opossum and raccoon. The women liked to adorn their bodies with necklaces, bracelets, and tattoos. (Engraving by Theodor de Bry, from Thomas Hariot's *A briefe and true report of the new found land of Virginia* [New York: Dover Publications, 1972])

Unusual parallel ditch features at Werowocomoco. (Werowocomoco Research Group)

Late in 1607, while exploring the Chickahominy River, Captain John Smith was captured and brought before Powhatan at the chief's principal residence Werowocomoco on the York River in present-day Gloucester County. Werowocomoco served as the capital of the paramount chiefdom during the height of Powhatan's power and his interaction with the English. After Powhatan freed Smith, the English visited Werowocomoco on several occasions in 1608 and 1609. In 1609 Powhatan decided the English were too close to him and moved further to the west. Today, archaeologists have established the location of Werowocomoco. A collaborative effort, lead by the landowner, archaeologists, and the Native American community, is investigating the site. Careful excavations have revealed well-preserved subsurface ditch and postmold features and extensive occupation across the site dating to the Late Woodland and European Contact periods.

The colonists kidnapped one of Powhatan's daughters, the famous Pocahontas. Pocahontas was the first Indian woman to marry an English colonist when she took John Rolfe for her husband in 1614. Rolfe introduced a mild West Indies strain of tobacco to Jamestown, which soon became the settlers' main crop. The years following the marriage were peaceful ones between the cultures. In 1615 Pocahontas gave birth to a son, Thomas Rolfe, and traveled to England with him, John, and a contingent of Indians representing the Virginia Company. Well received by the royal court, she was reluctant to return to Virginia. She became seriously ill and died in 1617.

During the first decade, encounters between colonists and Indians were often hostile. Seeing the land slowly taken from his people, Powhatan appealed to Captain John Smith in 1608. Meeting Smith at Werowocomoco, his headquarters, he said, "I, having seene the death of all my people thrice, and not one living of those 3 generations, but my selfe, I knowe the difference of peace and warre, better than any in my Countrie. . . . [W]hat will it availe you, to take that perforce, you may quietly have with love, or to destroy them that provide you food?" Powhatan died in 1618. Four years later, the people launched the first coordinated attack to expel the settlers, leading to a decade of intermittent warfare. The Indians tried a second time in 1644, but by then they were fewer in number and faced 15,000 colonists. Opechancanough, Wahunsunacock's brother, was the last Powhatan to exert control over Coastal Plain Algonquian subchiefdoms. After Opechancanough's death in 1646, the Powhatan chiefdom ceased to exist.

The once-mighty Powhatan chiefdom was reduced to a tributary status (it purchased peace and protection from the colonists) and lost all lands between the York and Blackwater rivers. In 1677 a major treaty was made with the colonists. The Indians along the coast lost their remaining land and were confined to small reservations for which an annual tribute was exacted by the colony.

Many of the tribal groups were reported extinct by 1722. The Rappahannock lost their reservation shortly after 1700; the Chickahominy lost theirs in 1718. These groups and the Nansemond, who sold their reservation in 1792, faded from public view. For reasons of sheer survival, they became invisible to the colonists. Only the Pamunkey, Mattaponi, and an Eastern Shore group kept reservations, although their land constantly shrank in size.

As some of the Indians adopted European lifestyles, they suffered more dissent within their districts. Some people wanted to keep the traditional ways, while others accepted white culture. Christianity and English gradually replaced Powhatan religion and language, two central aspects of their culture. The people still raised crops, hunted, and

WHAT WERE THEY LIKE?

The Lifestyles and Customs of the POWHATAN PEOPLE

From written accounts and archaeological findings, we can draw this picture of the traditions and events in the lives of the Powhatan people:

The woman looked at her son, who was sleeping. Tomorrow, he would begin the Huskinaw, and he would be lost to her as a child. Already 15, the boy would endure nine months of physical hardship, isolation in the forest, fasting, and concoctions that would cause hallucinations, or visions, with the bravest of the boys of age in the village. In the Huskinaw, the boys would forget their childhood as they prepared to become adults.

With a mixture of sadness and pride, the woman left the oval-shaped house. She was careful not to disturb the eight family members sleeping on animal skins lining low benches along the edges of the room. Among them were her husband, children, and mother. Outside in the moonlight, she could see the frame of a new house, the yehakin, being built near the river. The arched, circular frame was half covered with bark. This was the newest of 30 homes in the village.

Away from the village, she could see the quioccasan, which housed the priests and the preserved bodies of deceased chiefs. Here, the people of her social rank would gather at first light. The people of the lower status would hold a separate ceremony in a Dancing Face Circle, amidst a ring of carved posts.

The temple ceremony was a long one. The priests were striking in their headdresses of stuffed snake and weasel skins hanging down their painted faces. The boys and men painted their skin red as a means of magic to increase their power for the ceremony. The priests presented offerings of the harvest crops and game of the season. They prayed for the boys beginning the Huskinaw. Then, the boys were ceremonially abducted from their families and their training begun. They would return to the village as men, loyal only to the god Oke and to the village werowance, or chief.

The woman, the crenepo, offered her most precious shell beads on the altar for her son, and prayed that Oke, the fearful being who took good things away, would overlook him. She hoped that later, during the healing the shaman performed, her friend would receive a spell that would cure her aching chest.

Two weeks later, the woman laughed as everyone gathered for the wedding feast. A couple of high rank, a young man of 16 and a young woman of 13, were being married, and now there was a great celebration of food and dancing to the rhythmic music of drums, rattles, and flutes. Laid out on the ground before them were dishes of wild rice with mushrooms; roasted deer; a succotash of fish, maize, and beans; steamed oysters and crabs; tuckahoe bread; and hominy seasoned with bone grease.

The hem of the woman's fringed deerskin shirt, her finest garment, hung down almost to her knees. Her face and arms were adorned with tattoos of snakes and plum blossoms. Her hair, long and braided, reflected the fashion of married women. The wealthy women of the village were dressed in fringed skin mantles colored with designs of birds and animals. Headbands, crownlets, and necklaces of beads, feathers, freshwater pearls, dyed animals skins, and copper were their badges of distinction. The woman saw the chief among the crowd, a beautiful mantle of turkey feathers draped over him. His hair, hanging to his shoulders on one side, was completely shaved from the right side of his head.

Everyone was happy; the young man easily had won the approval of his bride and her parents, and his bride price of copper, shell beads, and deer skins to her parents was a handsome one. Ahone, the god who bestows all good things, had certainly blessed the union.

Two days later, the woman joined six other

mothers in the village to gather chestnuts, walnuts, hickory nuts, and acorns. Some of them carried containers made of clay, bark, and animal skins; others, baskets woven of pine needles, reeds, and hemp. Their children came, too, to help in the work. The children ran ahead, the youngest of them naked, the older girls wearing aprons. Two of the women traveled easily with babies bound to cradle boards. As one of the mothers called out to a child, the woman realized the child's birth name had been changed to reflect the child's growth and personality.

When the women and children returned to camp, it was quiet. Some of the men, the nemarough, had left to hunt deer and other game together. They painted their faces and shoulders red and smeared themselves with bear grease. Then they adorned their chests with necklaces of shell beads, animal teeth, and copper. They drove the game with small fires to a point of land along a river. Others of them, waiting in dugout canoes, would be close enough to shoot the entrapped deer and small mammals with bows and arrows. Sometimes, the best hunters went out alone, camouflaged with deerskins, to stalk and kill deer. Beaver, otter, and other small animals were taken with snares. Another group of men had gone off in large cypress canoes to fish all day and into the night. They caught perch, spot, and croaker in a variety of weirs, or traps, and on hooks. After hunting, the warriors gathered around a fire to celebrate and give thanks to the spirits. Pieces of tobacco were tossed into the fire as offerings.

A month later, the woman stood silently in shock and grief. The village was hidden in a haze of smoke, houses burning, women and children screaming. The settlers had attacked, and now 10 of her people were dead. The next day, the werowance of the village met with his council of advisers, the priest of the temple, and the priest of the perpetual fire to organize a special religious ceremony. The woman and all her people clung to their faith now, a powerful bond. According to their view of the universe, Oke was full of wrath, and the priests led the people in offerings of deer meat, dried tobacco, and bloodroot to appease him.

Then, they turned to the task of burying their dead. The woman wrapped the bodies of her sister and niece in mats. These were placed in a grave and covered with dirt. Joining other relatives and friends, the woman blackened her face with charcoal and lamented for the next full day. Other mourners gathered beneath scaffolds on which dead warriors had been wrapped and placed, higher than one could reach. Months later, after the flesh disappeared from the body, they would wrap the bones in a new mat and eventually bury them in the ground.

The woman thought of the village she had known all her life, now broken. She thought of the chiefs who led it, and who now, long dead, lay carefully preserved and wrapped in white skins on a platform in the temple, watched over by the priests. Surrounded by copper beads, hatchets, and other treasures, the dead leaders were tangible reminders of the village's past. "Who will be left?" the woman wondered. "Who among us will be left to plant the crops in spring?"

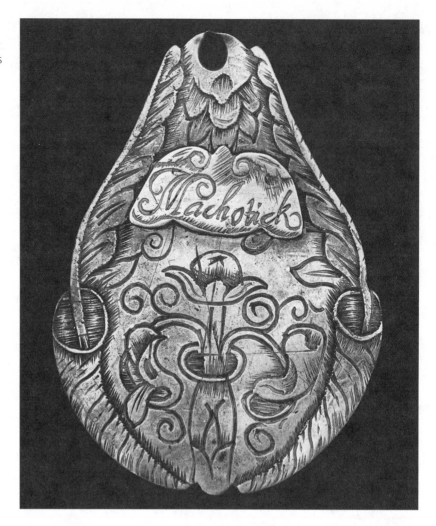

fished. Cash crops, like cotton, were added to their gardening. Livestock, such as chickens, cows, and hogs, became commonplace. Log and plank houses replaced the bark and mat-covered oval houses.

The Nottoway and Meherrin, two groups distinct from the Powhatans, lived in the interior Coastal Plain of Virginia. They spoke dialects of the Iroquoian language and lived along the Nottoway and Meherrin rivers. Like the coastal Algonquians, the people farmed and hunted, and their homes were similarly interspersed among fields of crops or within palisaded villages. Unlike members of the Powhatan chiefdom, however, the Nottoway and Meherrin lived as tribes in autonomous villages, with a local chief holding little sway beyond his village.

The Nottoway and Meherrin remained relatively undisturbed by the English settlements expanding from Jamestown. But, by 1650 the fur trade increased their contact with the settlers. Then in the 1677 treaty, they, too, lost their land and became tributaries of the colony. The Nottoway and Meherrin set up new settlements along the Nottoway River near Courtland in Southampton County. Claims by whites depleted their land, and the numbers of the two groups declined. By the late 1700s, the Meherrin had lost their reservation. The Nottoway still held theirs.

It appears from court records and related documents that the Indian populations in the Coastal Plain dropped from a height of 20,000 to about 1,800 by 1669 as a result of warfare and disease. Smallpox and measles, previously unknown to native inhabitants, infected entire villages.

Indians in the Piedmont

A number of Indian tribes that spoke dialects of the Siouan language lived in the Piedmont of Virginia. The Manahoac settled on the waters of the Rappahannock River west of Fredericksburg; the Monacan lived above the falls of the James River; and the Occaneechi and Saponi, above the falls of the Roanoke River. In general, the tribes in the Piedmont lived in autonomous hamlets and villages. They probably gathered to celebrate special times of the year, traded, intermarried, and met for deer hunts.

Little is known about these people; few early traders and travelers kept records. These sketchy pieces of information survive: John Smith in 1608 met a large group of Manahoac, who lived in at least seven villages to the west, at the falls of the Rappahannock River. The Manahoac were friends of the Monacan and enemies of the Powhatans. What happened to this tribe is not known. By 1667 no Indians were found in the area at all. The theory is that raiding Iroquois, disease, and contact with the colonists may have pushed the remaining Manahoac south to join the Monacan.

The first mention in records about the Monacan tribe comes from Captain John Smith. In 1608 he learned from a Powhatan informant about five Monacan towns west of the James River falls at present-day Richmond. A year later, Smith captured an Indian named Amoroleck, who told Smith that the people of the Piedmont avoided the English and were hostile to them on contact because, "They heard we were a people come from under the world to take their world from them."

Christopher Newport then led a group of men 40 miles west of the falls and discovered two of the villages. In 1670 German traveler John Lederer was commissioned by the governor of Virginia to explore the territory. Approaching one of the villages along the James, he was met with friendly volleys of firearms into the air. Almost 30 years later, a Huguenot colony of French Protestants settled in the vicinity of this abandoned village. Today, this area in Powhatan County retains the name of Monacan Town.

After leaving Monacan Town, Lederer proceeded to Sapon, a town of the Saponi people located in Charlotte County along the Roanoke River. Situated on high land with rich soil, the village had all the natural requirements for a pleasant settlement. Lederer wrote, "This nation is governed by an absolute monarch; the people of a high stature, warlike and rich. I saw great store of pearl unbored in their little temples, or oratories, which they had won amongst other spoyls from the Indians of Florida, and hold in as great esteem as we do."

Through the written records, we know very little about the Saponi. The Saponi believed in a supreme creator and subordinate deities. Their religion also embraced a belief in reincarnation. People who were evil in one life were given a second chance to "mend their manners."

Lederer advised traders to carry with them cloth, axes, hoes, knives, and scissors. Though the Indians were eager to purchase arms and ammunition, the colonial government outlawed such trade. For remote tribes, he wrote, the best articles to carry were small trinkets, copper, toys, beads, and bracelets. Lederer warned travelers to be careful when visiting the Saponi. A traveler was not to go into a house until invited. Then he was at first bound like a prisoner, a Saponi custom applied to both friends and enemies. Some experts believe this was a ritual of authority and trust. By analogy, many examples of rituals that affirm power are found in other cultures. A king in the act of knighting a subject, for example, uses a sword to convey the title. The sword, so wielded, could be used to tap the subject's shoulders, a sign of honor, or to cut off his head. Rather than an odd act of hostility, the ritual of binding a visitor could have been intended to set a similar tone of power and respect.

A year after Lederer's expedition, Robert Fallam and Captain Thomas Batts, under the commission of General Abraham Wood, left the James River near Petersburg and traveled west. The men arrived at Sapon Town, welcomed by the firing of guns and plenty of supplies. They went on a short distance and received another friendly reception

at the next village. Continuing beyond the Piedmont, they met with another warm greeting from the Totero people living in either the Roanoke or New River valleys.

Unable to withstand assaults by the Iroquois, the closely allied Saponi and Totero eventually left all their villages and moved south, joining their friends, the Occaneechi, or east, to be closer to the English at Fort Henry.

According to John Lederer's reports, the Occaneechi people lived in an island in the Roanoke River near Clarksville. Two chiefs governed the Occaneechi, one presiding in war, the other in peace. From 500 miles away, other tribes came to the village to trade, making the island a great regional center. The Occaneechi language served as the common tongue of all the tribes of the area.

Among his observations about the tribe, Lederer noted: "An account of time, and other things, they keep on a string or leather thong tied in knots of several colours. I took particular notice of small wheels serving for this purpose amongst the Onenocks, because I have heard that the Mexicans use the same."

In 1676 the Susquehannock of Pennsylvania contacted the Occaneechi to expand their trade with the Europeans. The Occaneechi received

European traders used commonplace items such as beads, trinkets, brass kettles, and pewter spoons as barter with Virginia Indians.

them, but hostilities arose and the Susquehannock were driven from the island.

In the same year, Nathaniel Bacon led a group of Virginia colonists in a revolt against the government. He accused Governor William Berkeley of doing nothing to prevent the ongoing Indian raids in the western part of the state. He also charged Berkeley with granting political favors to allies and friends. Bacon and his discontented followers saw large plantation owners holding huge land grants, Indians roaming vast tracts, and themselves without. When Berkeley was removed as governor for a brief period, the rebels pursued the Susquehannock and defeated them with the help of the Occaneechi. Then, the colonists turned on the Occaneechi, killing over 50 people. The Occaneechi soon fled south into North Carolina along with the Saponi and Totero. Soon after, Bacon died of dysentery, the "bloody flux." Berkeley regained power as governor.

Probably around 1716, the Saponi, Totero, and Occaneechi left North Carolina for Fort Christanna in Brunswick County, Virginia, in a move to maintain closer trade relations with Virginians and to sever ties with Charleston traders who tried to control them. Governor Spotswood directed that a school be built for the Indian children and a trading center be established. The Indians' presence there provided a barrier between hostile tribes to the south and the Virginia settlements. In 1722 a general peace was made between the Iroquois and the Virginia and Carolina Indians. Around 1740, the Saponi, Totero, and Occaneechi moved north with the permission of the Iroquois and settled in Pennsylvania.

In 1833 a group of Piedmont Indians purchased 400 acres of land on Bear Mountain in Amherst County. They established a small enclave that continues to exist. Today their descendants are known as the Monacan Indian Nation.

Native Americans in the Mountains

Little is known from the written record of the Indians who lived in the mountains of western Virginia. John Lederer was the first European to view the Shenandoah Valley from the Blue Ridge when his party traveled up the headwaters of the Rappahannock River. The Robert Fallam and Thomas Batts expedition of 1671 marked the first contact with the Totero people living in either the Roanoke or New River valleys. By 1706, when Louis Michel, a French Swiss traveler, proceeded up the Shenandoah River to a point near Edinburg, he noted that "All this country is uninhabited except by some Indians." The area was devoid of any permanent settlements, with only hunting parties of Shawnee, Susquehannock, and Iroquois moving through. Why was the area barren of villages? No records remain to tell us, although conflict with the settlers and the spread of European diseases through the villages certainly took their toll.

The early colonial times were turbulent for the Indians of the Shenandoah Valley. In only a few generations the Susquehannock, who wanted to control the area's European fur trade, forced the Shawnee out. The Iroquois in turn forced the Susquehannock out. In 1744, many tribes gathered in a council meeting at Lancaster, Pennsylvania. The speaker for the Iroquois league asserted that all the world knew that they had conquered the tribes formerly living on the Susquehannock and Potomac rivers and at the back of the Blue Ridge (the Shenandoah Valley).

The French and Indian War (1754–63) started over competing claims to the Ohio territory between the British and French. Upon attack, settlers sought refuge at nearby forts that the colonial government constructed. The forts formed a chain along the Valley and the eastern front of the Blue Ridge. Many settlers who lived in this area fled to the safety of the Piedmont and Tidewater regions of Virginia and the Carolinas. Those who stayed risked attack, death, or capture by the Shawnee from the Ohio Valley, later led by the great Indian chief Tecumseh.

By the time enough Europeans came to set up towns, southwestern Virginia had become another region void of Indian villages. The only natives sighted were hunting and trading groups of Cherokee and Shawnee passing through.

Thomas Walker, a physician who became surveyor for the Royal Land Company, never saw any Indians or any evidence of a village in his 1750 expedition through Southwest Virginia. Twice, however, he came across Indian tracks on the trail. When he reached Long Island in the Holston River at Kingsport, Tennessee, he described this abandoned village, which may have been Cherokee: "In the Fork between Holston's and the North River, are five Indian Houses built with logs and covered with bark, and there were an abundance of Bones, some whole Pots and Pans, some broken and many pieces of mats and Cloth." Long Island was connected to events relating to the Cherokee. According to tradition, it was an ancient treaty ground.

The Cherokee lived in the mountains of North Carolina, Georgia, Tennessee, and extreme southwestern Virginia. In towns along the rivers, they built homes made from vertical poles set in the ground, between which were woven slender branches. They plastered the branches with clay to form walls. Low platforms along the walls served as beds. To shelter themselves during the winter months, they built small windowless earthen lodges that were warmed by a small fire.

Cherokee children were considered part of their mother's family, typical of the matrilineal system. Young men who married lived with their in-laws. People who were related through their mother's side of the family belonged to the same clan. There were seven clans: the Wolf, Deer, Bird, Wild Potato, Red Paint, Blue, and Twisters.

The older men, who sat in a council led by the head priest, ruled each Cherokee village. The Cherokee had no chief like the Powhatan. The whole village could attend a council meeting, with the people seated by clan around the large council house. Decisions were reached by consensus.

Two rituals were performed each year. The Green Corn Feast, a time of giving thanks for the harvest, was held when the corn ripened. In the other ritual, held in late fall, the village was purified and reunited by cleaning the council house and putting out all the hearth fires in the village, even the sacred fire in the council house. A new sacred fire was lit and from it all the homes rekindled their hearths. The people fasted and bathed and forgave most wrongs done to them during the last year. Thus, they entered the new year with their environment, spirit, and social relationships made fresh and new.

The Cherokee liked to play stick ball, a game similar to lacrosse. One village often competed against another on a huge field. The game was so rough that it was considered a substitute for warfare. The Cherokee prized bravery; fierce sport and warring were two means by which a man could prove his worth.

Even after many years of conflict and military defeat during the French and Indian War and the American Revolution, the Cherokee still managed to remain a visible political and cultural entity. But because of the loss of land and their increasing dependence on the white economic system, they changed their lifeways of hunting, farming, and trading. Cherokee men learned how to fence fields and plow, the women how to spin and weave cotton. They became familiar with gristmills and the craft of blacksmithing. Cherokee leaders, in particular, favored the "civilization" program because they knew that an English education would enable the next generation to survive and thrive.

Despite the Cherokee accomplishments, whites still demanded their land. When gold was discovered on Cherokee lands in 1828, the pressure to remove the Cherokee increased. The Cherokee were moved west to present-day Oklahoma in 1838. Of the 16,000 who started on the "Trail of Tears," 4,000 died.

Scattered families of Cherokee remained in Tennessee and Georgia, and an entire Indian community, known as the Oconaluftee Cherokee, remained in North Carolina. The Qualla Boundary, the Cherokee reservation of today, consists of land the Cherokee bought before the Civil War.

Preston Adkins, former director and current member of the Chickahominy Tribal Dancers, keeps colorful traditions alive. (*Richmond Times-Dispatch*)

Virginia Indians, 1800s to the Present

As I look at my children and reflect upon their growing years, I am proud they have grown up strong like the mighty Oak Tree. I am proud they withstood the thrashing winds of rejection and the trail of bitter tears. I am proud the seed of self-respect our people have long sought took root; and like a flower they have blossomed to spread out and start a new generation.
—Daniel Fortune, Elder Councilman, Rappahannock Indian Tribe

In the 1800s, the prevailing white culture wanted to push the Indians off their homelands and control the territory. Pressure was brought to remove each of the four remaining reservations and end the people's legal status as tribes. This policy meant dividing, with the Indians' consent, all of a reservation among each of its members and removing all state services to the tribe. Whites assumed that the Indians would eventually sell their lands to neighboring white farms and disappear as a tribal group. The Gingaskin Reservation on the Eastern Shore was legally subdivided in 1813. Unable to withstand legal pressure and being very poor, the people sold their land for profit. By 1850 all of the original Gingaskin Reservation was in white hands. The last parcel of the Nottoway Reservation was divided in 1878, although many families held onto their land until well into the 20th century. The Pamunkey and Mattaponi, the last two reservations, withstood attempts at termination. Though the people were poor, they maintained their tribal structure and treaties with the Commonwealth. Today, their reservations are two of the oldest in the nation, symbols of a people who refused to give up. Their example has been an incentive for the nonreservation Indian people, who, around the time of the Civil War, began to resurface as identified enclaves. In the early 1900s, these enclaves reorganized into tribes.

After the Civil War, the reservation tribes sought to rebuild their cultural identity and unity. They also sought to improve their image among the people of the Commonwealth. In the late 1800s, for example, the Pamunkey tribe staged plays for 30 years recounting the story of Pocahontas and John Smith to remind white Virginia of the debt it owed to the Powhatan people for saving Jamestown. The play also carried the message that Powhatan's descendants were still alive and not ashamed of their heritage. Following the cessation of these plays, the Mattaponi tribe continued to rebuild its cultural identity by going into the business community and into school systems, teaching the history of the Powhatan culture.

During the 19th century, state laws restricted a Virginia Indian's ability to travel, testify in court, and inherit property. Divisions between white, black, and Indian cultures resulted in rigid, three-way segregation in schools and churches. The move by Indian descendants to form tribes was seen as a threat by some people who wanted to keep the white race "pure." Led by Dr. Walter A. Plecker, a group called the Anglo-Saxon Club of America prevailed upon the General Assembly to pass the Racial Integrity Law in 1924. According to this law, in matters of births, marriages, and deaths, the Virginia Bureau of Vital Statistics recognized only two races—white and black. Recent newspaper accounts and books by historians hold that Dr. Plecker, as registrar of the Bureau of Vital Statistics from 1912 to 1946, waged a one-man war against Virginia's Indians, in efforts some call "documentary genocide." U.S. Census figures in 1930 showed 779 Native Americans living in Virginia; by 1940, the figure dropped to 198. In effect, people of Indian descent did not exist. A warning was attached to Indian birth and death certificates stating that the person would be classified as "Colored" and treated accordingly. Not until 1972 did it become illegal for the Bureau of Vital Statistics to send this warning with each certificate.

After 1924 the Indians of Virginia legally could not attend white schools or marry whites. They had to wed in churches outside the state to be recorded as Indian. They lost the means to document through state and county records Virginia Indian populations, movements of families, or family ties. Lloyd Johns, a Monacan, tells how the effects of this documentary genocide remain today: "I looked up my family records and found that my grandparents were labeled first white, then Indian, then Indian mix, then some Negro thrown in. Very strange progression! I wondered why the change. Even brothers and sisters were labeled differently. Seems like someone wanted to do away with the

Indians." Today some Indians bitterly remember this period when their cultural identity was nearly smothered.

Katie Southward, at the Pamunkey Indian reservation, creates pottery in the tradition of her ancestors. (Pamunkey Indian Tribe)

Since the Indians were not accepted into white or black churches and schools, they opened their own. Today, all of the tribes have churches, most of which are Southern Baptist. Two exceptions include the Nansemond church, which is United Methodist, and the Monacan mission, which is Episcopalian.

The Indian schools in Virginia did not go beyond the seventh grade until the late 1950s. To finish high school, young reservation Indian students were sent by the Commonwealth to Bacone College in Muskogee, Oklahoma, or the federal boarding school in Cherokee, North Carolina. At the college level, no efforts were made to include Indian students in the racially mixed Hampton Institute, which educated many students from tribes outside of Virginia. Still, the Indians were motivated to succeed. By the 1950s, the reservations were producing radio announcers and accountants. The requirements for school integra-

Shirley "Little Dove" Custalow McGowan travels across the state to schools, community groups, and festivals, teaching the heritage and lifeways of the Powhatan people. (*Newport News Daily Press*)

tion during the Civil Rights movement of the 1960s removed the need for Indian students to leave the state to further their education. Some Indian communities objected to integration; they wished to maintain their separate identity.

The Civil Rights movement promoted opportunities for education and employment for the Indians as well as other minorities. By 1964 the first Powhatan Indian physician from the Mattaponi reservation had graduated from the Medical College of Virginia. After the movement was actively in force, doors opened for the more rapid advancement of Indian people into all professional levels of society. In the last one hundred years, the Indian people of Virginia have entered fully into the social and economic life of the Commonwealth.

Many activities among Virginia's Indians are continuing to build a strong sense of identity among the tribes. Recently nonreservation tribal centers have emerged as symbols of unity, similar to those on the reservations. The people use the centers to hold tribal councils, dances, dinners, and exhibits. They meet in the centers to conduct adult education classes and run craft guilds. Dance groups, such as the Rappahannock American Indian Dancers, Chickahominy Redmen Dancers, and River of High Banks Drum from Mattaponi, preserve the heritage of Virginia tribal dancing and actively teach native dances to children and adults. Increasingly popular tribal powwows enable Virginia Indian tribes to meet with the public and demonstrate crafts, dances, and share oral histories.

In its concern over education, a group of seven tribes formed The United Indians of Virginia (UIV) in 1988. The UIV set up a scholarship fund for young adults. Other goals included coordinating cultural events and economic and social development efforts. The council operates by consensus, with officers elected by the eight tribes that now are included in the UIV.

The Virginia Council on Indians was established by an act of the General Assembly in 1983. The state officially recognized six tribes in that same session: the Chickahominy, Eastern Chickahominy, Mattaponi, Pamunkey, Rappahannock, and Upper Mattaponi. With the endorsement of the council, the General Assembly subsequently recognized the Nansemond Tribe in 1985 and the Monacan Tribe in 1989. Presently the council is composed of 18 members: one member from each of the state recognized tribes, five Indian-at-large members, one citizen-at-large member, and four members of the General Assembly. The council is affiliated with the secretary of natural resources in the governor's cabinet. It informs and advises the governor, General Assembly, and state agencies on issues of interest to Indians in Virginia, such as the educational Standards of Learning, archaeology on Native American sites, and the respectful treatment of Native remains and funerary objects. The council also serves as a resource to Native Americans throughout Virginia, as well as to the general public for questions about the Virginia Indians.

During the 1990s, the Virginia tribes pursued federal recognition through the Bureau of Indian Affairs. After the bureau indicated that it could take decades to receive administrative recognition, the tribes in 1999 formed VITAL, the Virginia Indian Tribal Alliance for Life. VITAL decided to pursue congressional recognition. Since 2000, bills have been introduced to both houses of the United State Congress seeking federal acknowledgement for Virginia tribes. VITAL recognizes the right of Indian tribes to self-government and supports tribal sovereignty and self-determination. VITAL is also a research and education organization dedicated to a wider understanding and appreciation of the ideas and knowledge of indigenous peoples, and to the social, economic, and political realities of the American Indians of the Commonwealth of Virginia.

At the same time Virginia Indians' self-images are changing, the popular view of them is shifting, too. More people recognize that the world has inherited from the Indians a legacy of many valuable foods, tools, and words. Corn, one of the world's most precious foods, is one of their gifts. They also raised squash, beans, and tobacco. The early Native Americans invented canoes, smoking pipes, and snowshoes. The names of many Virginia counties, cities, towns, and roads are Indian names, such as Quioccasan, Powhite, Appomattox, Rappahannock, and Tuckahoe. Common words, including moccasin, raccoon, hickory, moose, chipmunk, and skunk are also Indian words.

Public school curricula are now being recast to include the perspective of indigenous peoples and more complete and accurate information about their histories and their cultures. Thought-provoking films and books are making people in general aware of the beliefs of the Indians and their ways of adapting to the environment. As Oliver Perry stated, "So much has been gained. . . . We feel that God made all people and has brought them together in today's culture. In this, we all want to live together and yet maintain our separate identities. That's what we're working toward—to make Virginia as God intends it to be—all mankind living in harmony. Perhaps in the future all people might be more compassionate and understanding than they have been in the past."

Indian Tribes in Virginia Today

Chickahominy

The Chickahominy Indian Tribe was among those that witnessed the coming of the colonists in 1607. The tribe's territory ranged from Jamestown to the "fall line," near present-day Richmond. The tribe, ruled by a council of elders, was considered an ally of the Powhatan and his chiefdom. The Treaty of 1614 between the Chickahominy and the colonists provided that the Chickahominy would supply 300–400 bowman to fight the Spanish, if necessary. It appears that the colonists were more afraid of the Spanish than they were of the Indians.

When the Indians were sent to "Pamunkey Neck" in what is now King William County, the Chickahominy joined the other tribes. After 1718, the Indians were forced off that reservation. The Chickahominy tribe moved back to the homeland in present-day Charles City and New Kent counties. The tribe reorganized in 1900, led by a chief, assistant chief, and a tribal council.

This tribe is Virginia's largest, with approximately 1,000 members. Its 25,000-acre enclave includes a tract on state Route 602 that holds Samaria Baptist Church, the former Samaria Indian School that has been remodeled and is now part of the church, and a tribal center for meetings and recreation. Politically active, the tribe has placed members on the county school board, the planning commission, and in local government offices. The tribe was recognized by the Commonwealth of Virginia in 1983.

Eastern Chickahominy

Located in New Kent County, 25 miles east of Richmond, the eastern division of the tribe has 150 members. It was formed in 1925 after a split with the Chickahominy Indian Tribe. Now it is incorporated as a tax-exempt organization to serve the educational, religious, and other needs of its members.

Mattaponi

This King William County tribe of some 100 members lives on a reservation along the Mattaponi River near West Point, Virginia. The tribe traces its history back to the Powhatan chiefdom that greeted the settlers in 1607. At that time, the Mattaponi, along with other original Powhatan tribes, were visited by Captain John Smith. The reservation dates back to 1658 and is one of the oldest in the United States. While many other tribes have been displaced, the Mattaponi have persisted as a result of their strong traditions, ceremonies, and leadership qualities, which have held the tribe together. Today, the Mattaponi's pride in their cultural heritage is greater than ever. Shad have always been both a staple in the Mattaponi diet and the center of their culture. These traditions continue as the Mattaponi people work in harmony with the land and the river at the tribal fish hatchery and marine resource center.

The late Chief Webster Custalow, of the Mattaponi Indian Tribe. (*Richmond Times-Dispatch*)

Monacan

The Monacan live in the Piedmont region, west of the other state-recognized tribes. Along with other Siouan-speaking tribes such as the Saponi, Tutelo, and Mannahoac, they once occupied most of the western half of what is now Virginia. Early settlers wrote little about them, both because they were enemies of the Powhatan and because they chose not to interact with the English.

The Monacan are self-governed by a chief, assistant chief, and tribal council elected by tribal members. The population today is more than 1,400 people. The tribe is revitalizing its cultural traditions and language. To preserve its heritage, the tribe developed its own museum, which displays both artifacts and modern exhibits. The museum is located at the site of Bear Mountain, the spiritual center of the Monacan people and the location of an Episcopal mission church established in 1908. Today, the old log cabin schoolhouse is a restored historic landmark, and the tribe operates a food bank, elder program, youth cultural program, and many other projects that benefit tribal members.

Nansemond

At the time of the Jamestown settlement in 1607, the Nansemond tribe was located in the general area of Reeds Ferry near Chuckatuck, in the current City of Suffolk. The chief lived near Dumpling Island, where he kept his religious houses. The tribe had a population of approximately 850, with 200 bowmen. In 1608 Jamestown was suffering from a severe food shortage. John Smith attempted to bargain with the Nansemond Indians with varying degrees of success. The endeavor ended in open hostilities. The Nansemond have been said to have become the granary of the early colonists. As increasing numbers of settlers moved up the Nansemond River, the Nansemond Indians relocated their reservation and tribal land several times. They sold their last 300 acres, located on the Nottoway River in Southampton County, in 1792.

One group of Christianized Nansemond moved and settled in the Bowers Hill, Deep Creek, area on the fringe of the Great Dismal Swamp in the late 1600s. Their descendants still live in that location and surrounding areas.

It is the Christianized Nansemond from whom the present Nansemond Indian Tribe is descended. The tribe holds its meetings at the Indiana United Methodist Church, founded in 1850 as a mission for the Nansemond Indians. The Nansemond Indian Tribe, as one of the remaining tribes of the Powhatan, received official recognition from the General Assembly and the Commonwealth of Virginia in 1985.

Pamunkey

One hundred members of this tribe live on a reservation in King William County on the Pamunkey River. The Pamunkey Indians were one of the most powerful of the tribes in the Powhatan chiefdom. The chiefdom consisted of approximately 32 districts and over 14,000 people under the leadership of the ruling Powhatan. The Powhatan territory encompassed most of the Coastal Plain of Virginia from the North Carolina border to Washington, D.C. Chief Powhatan and his famous daughter Pocahontas lived among the Pamunkey.

The Pamunkey enjoy the distinction of being one of the tribes east of the Mississippi that has practiced the art of pottery making continuously since aboriginal times. Through the school year, school children who are studying Indian life visit the reservation, purchase souvenirs, and join the Indians in traditional native dances.

Rappahannock

In 1607 the Rappahannock were the dominant tribe of the Rappahannock River Valley, maintaining 13 villages along the north and south banks of the river that bears their name. The king's town was located at "Cat Point Creek," or "Dancing Point" as known to the tribe, near present-day Warsaw. It was here, in December 1607, that the Rappahannock first met Captain John Smith. He was brought to see the king at "Toppahanoke" while Opechancanough held him captive. Over the next 40 years, English settlement expanded up the Rappahannock River. By 1655 the Rappahannock had abandoned their village sites along the river and established themselves inland along the Totuskey Creek. In 1672, responding to Susquehannock attacks, the Rappahannock moved further south and established a new fortified village on the ridge between the Mattaponi and Rappahannock rivers, about three miles northwest of the modern day Tappahannock. By "an order of council dated November 25, 1682, it was directed that 4,000 acres of land should be laid out for the Rappahannock Indians about the town where they dwelt." The next year the Rappahannock fort was threatened by Iroquoian war parties raiding the Virginia frontier.

To protect the Rappahannock and their English neighbors, Colonel William Byrd negotiated a settlement with the Iroquois, and the

Virginia assembly ordered the Tappahannock town to be relocated at Portobago Indian Town, in present-day Essex County. The Rappahannock remained at Portobago for some 20 years before Lieutenant Colonel Richard Covington escorted them back to their lands in King and Queen and Essex counties, where their descendants have remained until the present. The Rappahannock incorporated with the state in 1921. Members of the tribe established the Rappahannock Indian Baptist Church for their community in 1964. In 1983 the Rappahannock gained official recognition from the Commonwealth as one of Virginia's historic tribes. In 1998 they elected the first woman chief to lead in Virginia since the 1700s, Chief G. Anne Richardson. The tribe is a nonprofit organization, and its assets include 140.5 acres of land and the Rappahannock Cultural Center in Indian Neck, King and Queen County. The Rappahannock host their traditional harvest festival and powwow annually in October at the cultural center. Their mission is to preserve Rappahannock culture and social/political structures, establish a tribal land/trust, and implement housing and economic development projects while educating the public on the rich contributions they have made and continue to make to Virginia and the nation.

Upper Mattaponi

The Upper Mattaponi Indian Tribe resides near the upper reaches of the Mattaponi River near Aylett in present-day King William County. In 1608 Captain John Smith identified the village of Passaunkack at the location of the present-day Upper Mattaponi. The 1670 map by Augustin Herrman shows several Indian houses along the Upper Mattaponi River directly at the location of the Upper Mattaponi people, identifying that region as Indian land. From 1702 to 1727, an official interpreter of the Indians to the British named James Adams lived near this area, and an 1863 Civil War map also identifies the area as Indian land. During that era, the local Indians were known as the Adamstown band, because so many of them had the last name Adams. In 1921 the Adamstown Indians officially became the Upper Mattaponi Indian Tribe.

In the late 1800s, the Upper Mattaponi had a school that existed for a short time, and a one-room structure was built in 1919. This school served the Upper Mattaponi until 1952, when a modern brick structure replaced it. This structure still stands and has been recognized for its historic significance. Today, the building also serves as the tribal center. Next door to the school is the Indian View Baptist Church, which was built in 1942 and which serves as the home church for many of the Upper Mattaponi people.

Today the Upper Mattaponi also own 32 acres of land and have been working diligently toward federal acknowledgment. They are a proud, humble people, with strong character and values, much optimism, and hope for the future.

Protection of Native American Archaeological Sites

Most of what we know about the first people before 1607 archaeologists have gleaned from Indian sites across the state. It is important to understand the serious and urgent need to preserve these sites. Many are in danger of being destroyed. Each site is unique in the information it contains. It cannot be replaced. When sites are damaged before archaeologists can study them, the information—and our understanding of the past—is lost forever.

Sites are destroyed in two ways: by nature and by humans. Natural forces wear down the earth's surface and gradually remove traces of any markings, postmolds, and material remains. Normally, exposed areas on high or sloping ground are the ones most battered by wind, rain, and water. Rivers and the Atlantic Ocean also slowly erode land and can damage sites. In fact, the average shoreline erosion rate for Virginia is a staggering one foot per year. This destructive process increases during major storms and hurricanes.

Humans can unwittingly destroy sites in the normal course of constructing houses, roads, lakes, and factories. Even the very important work of cultivating fields to raise food may harm sites through soil erosion. Since 1607, soil loss in Virginia resulting from plowing has averaged five inches, with some areas losing as much as two feet. A survey of an area before any building or farming begins can reveal the hidden assets beneath the ground. In some cases, developers have included newly discovered sites in their project plans. Some sites have become the focal point of a residential neighborhood or district, adding richly to a community's sense of the past.

Unfortunately, humans also destroy sites through acts of collecting. Artifact collectors often dig for treasure, hoping to discover something of great value. They sell the objects to make money or keep them to

build a collection. Collectors place no cultural value on the site from which they are taking the artifacts. While they dig for treasure, they destroy the real find—Native American hamlets, villages, and tribal centers that hold clues to our shared past. In just a few generations, the archaeological remains of 17,000 years of Indian activity could be nearly destroyed by progress and collecting.

Several laws help to protect Indian sites in Virginia. The federal Archaeological Resource Protection Act (1979) and the Virginia Antiquities Act (1977) prohibit removing without a permit all cultural resources on government property. The Virginia Cave Act (1979) bars excavation without a permit within all caves and rockshelters. State burial laws prohibit removing, without a permit or court order, all human burials, regardless of age or cultural affiliation.

The National Historic Preservation Act (1966) requires review by archaeologists on federally funded, assisted, or permitted projects to consider their impact on important archaeological sites. Often this review results in the excavation of a site before construction, or altering the project plans to avoid the site. However, the fate of most archaeological sites is determined by private development, to which few if any guidelines apply.

Including Indian sites on the Virginia Landmarks Register and on the National Register of Historic Places can also encourage their protection. These two registers do not regulate property owners, but they do encourage preservation of sites by calling attention to their special significance. The Crab Orchard Site, Ely Mound, Daugherty's Cave, Cactus Hill, and Thunderbird Paleoindian Site, all mentioned earlier, are examples of sites listed on these two registers. Property owners wishing to provide for the permanent protection of significant sites can do so by granting a protective easement to the Commonwealth of Virginia or to some other appropriate organization. Much of the Thunderbird site is protected in this manner.

Archaeological restoration preserves cultural artifacts, such as this large ceramic storage vessel, and enables us to learn from the past.

Here is what you can do to help protect our irreplaceable cultural resources:

1. Don't dig

Each site is a unique page in the story of Virginia Indians. Whether it is for curiosity or greed, digging for any reason destroys the context of a site. If the site is skillfully excavated under the eye of an archaeologist,

Discovery of a Native American oval house in a contemporary Tidewater neighborhood led to its excavation and study. Some developers opt to include such sites in neighborhoods or industrial parks to preserve a sense of history for future residents.

that unique page can be read, recorded, and retold. If that careful reading does not happen during excavation, then the site and its story are both gone forever; the recovered artifacts may look interesting, but their true meaning will remain obscure.

2. Learn how to identify and report sites

We can't preserve or study sites unless we know where they are. The Department of Historic Resources maintains a list of sites all over Virginia. These lists can be used by researchers and by people making decisions about building roads and other large developments. Both the department and the Archeological Society of Virginia can help you report sites.

3. Participate in decisions that affect archaeological sites

Local governments and state and federal agencies that own property or that make decisions about zoning, permits, construction, highways, and similar activities that may damage archaeological sites usually have a way in which citizens can participate in those decisions. If you contact your local government or the individual agency to learn about these procedures, you can let the decision makers know that you think archaeological sites are important. This would also be a good project for a history or civics class as a way to learn how local governments make decisions.

4. Join the Archeological Society of Virginia

This statewide organization is made up of people like you who want to learn about Virginia's history and prehistory by studying and protecting archaeological sites. The society publishes a newsletter and a quarterly bulletin with reports on archaeological sites and issues, and it sponsors many events each year. There may be a local chapter in your area with even more things to do.

5. Organize a Virginia Archaeology Month event in your community

Find a local museum, library, school, historical society, or other organization to sponsor an exhibit, lecture, or other event. The Department of Historic Resources or the Archeological Society of Virginia can help you develop ideas and find speakers. They can also send posters and other information to use at the event.

6. Volunteer to work on a site or in a lab

Many ongoing archaeological projects welcome volunteer assistance, especially to help process artifacts in the laboratory. Since digging—even by archaeologists—destroys the site being studied, make sure that the project you choose is one that is conducted to meet state and federal standards. The Department of Historic Resources maintains information on some of the projects that welcome volunteers. Contact the individual project sponsor for information on volunteer programs and schedules.

7. Read

The more you know about what can be learned through careful archaeological study and analysis, the better you can explain to others the importance of protecting archaeological sites. Both the Department of Historic Resources and the Archeological Society of Virginia publish books and reports about Virginia archaeology. Public and college libraries are good sources for both books and magazines about archaeology. You can also find *Archaeology* magazine in many bookstores.

8. Join the Archaeological Conservancy

The Conservancy actively seeks sites in Virginia to protect until they can be properly and conservatively researched. Membership in the Conservancy includes a subscription to *American Archaeology* magazine.

Glossary

Archaeology The scientific study of past cultures through the systematic recovery and interpretation of their material remains.

Archaic period An archaeological period dating in Virginia from 8000 to 1200 BC.

Artifact A general term for tools, weapons, utensils, and other items made by man.

Atlatl An Aztec word for spear thrower. Spanish accounts described warriors throwing spears with great force, enough to penetrate iron armor. Elaborately carved stones occasionally were attached to the atlatl.

Band A form of sociopolitical organization in which a few related families lived together for mutual support and protection.

Beringia An immense tundra exposed before 8000 BC in the region of the Bering Sea at the time of lower sea levels during the Pleistocene.

Celt A narrow, wedge-shaped stone tool without a groove used as an adze or ax.

Chiefdom A form of sociopolitical organization in which the society was ranked. All the villages in a region were united and led by one very powerful person or family whose authority was inherited.

Cultigens Plants, such as sunflowers, gourds, squash, corn, beans, and tobacco, that were raised and harvested by Indians.

Culture All of the patterns of living humans have created in adapting to their environment and that are transmitted from one generation to another through means of behavior, symbols, and artifacts.

Ethnography The descriptive study of the cultural characteristics of diverse human societies, especially in reference to nonliterate people.

Hafted State of being affixed to a wooden or bone handle or shaft using a wrapping such as sinew or rawhide.

Mammoth and mastodon Two types of elephants that became extinct at the end of the Pleistocene. The first was a grazing animal that lived in grasslands, and the second was a browsing animal that lived in forests.

Matrilineal System in which descent and inheritance are passed through the mother rather than through the father.

Mississippian culture A highly sophisticated Indian culture dating to AD 900–1600. It was located in the Midwest along the Mississippi River and in the Southeastern North American continent.

Mortar A flat stone upon which seeds and nuts were crushed, using a hand stone or pestle.

Mortuary house A structure in which Indians placed the bodies of deceased relatives.

Native American An alternative term for the American Indians.

Ossuary A communal grave in which the Indians buried the bones of the dead that previously were either placed in a mortuary house or buried in the ground and exhumed.

Paleoindian period The oldest period of Indian occupation, 15,000–8000 BC, in Virginia.

Palisade A row of tall posts forming a fence, usually erected for demarcation or protection.

Pictographs Designs drawn by Indians with pigment on stone.

Pleistocene The last ice age, ending around 8000 BC, when great ice sheets or glaciers covered much of the North American continent.

Postmold The evidence in the ground of a post after the wood has rotted away. It is identified by the darker color of the soil.

Projectile point A general term referring to the stone head or point of a knife, arrow, or spear.

Shell midden A thick refuse heap of shell that accumulated where Indians gathered shellfish for food.

Slash-and-burn The technique of quickly clearing the forest by cutting and burning the trees and bushes. The resulting ash added nutrients to the soil for the raising of crops.

Soapstone A soft stone used by Indians to carve vessels during the Late Archaic period and to make ornaments during the Woodland period.

Stratigraphy The successive layers of natural and cultural levels at a site.

Temper Crushed material, such as stone or shell, that was added to clay to reduce shrinkage and cracking during the drying and firing of ceramic vessels.

Tribe A form of sociopolitical organization where one village was autonomous from another and where leadership was not inherited but acquired through merit.

Tuckahoe root A plant that grows in freshwater marshes in the Coastal Plain. Indians used its large, starchy root as a source of food.

Woodland period The last archaeological period for Indians, dating in Virginia from 1200 BC to AD 1600.

Public Resources

Virginia Council on Indians
P.O. Box 1475
Richmond, VA 23218
(804) 225-2084
indians.vipnet.org
vci@governor.virginia.gov

Virginia Department of Historic Resources
2801 Kensington Avenue
Richmond, VA 23221
(804) 367-2323
www.dhr.virginia.gov
Atlas of Virginia Archaeology
www.dhr.virginia.gov/arch_NET/
arch_NET3.htm

American Indian Resource Center
College of William and Mary
Williamsburg, VA 23185
(757) 221-1112
www.wm.edu/airc

Archeological Society of Virginia
P.O. Box 70395
Richmond, VA 23255-0395
asv-archeology.org

Department of Anthropology
College of William and Mary
Williamsburg, VA 23185
(757) 221-105
www.wm.edu/anthropology
powhatan.wm.edu

Department of Anthropology
University of Virginia
Charlottesville, VA 22903
(434) 924-7044
www.virginia.edu/anthropology

Department of Sociology and Anthropology
James Madison University
Harrisonburg, VA 22807
(540) 568-6171
www.jmu.edu/sociology

Center for Historic Preservation
University of Mary Washington
Fredericksburg, VA 22401-5358
(540) 654-1131
www.umw.edu/historicpreservation

Cultural Resources
Fairfax County Park Authority
2855 Annandale Road
Falls Church, VA 22042
(703) 534-3881

National Forest Service
5162 Valleypointe Parkway
Roanoke, VA 24019
(540) 265-5211

Monacan Village at Natural Bridge
P.O. Box 57
Natural Bridge, VA 24578
(800) 533-1410
www.naturalbridgeva.com

Monacan Ancestral Museum
2009 Kenmore Road
Amherst, VA 24521
(434) 946-5391
www.monacannation.com

First Landing State Park Visitor Center
2500 Shore Drive
Virginia Beach, VA 23451-1415
(757) 412-2300
www.dcr.virginia.gov/state_parks/fir.shtml

Pamunkey Indian Museum
175 Lay Landing Road
Pamunkey Indian Reservation
King William, VA 23086
(804) 843-4792
www.baylink.org/pamunkey

Amazement Square
27 Ninth Street
Lynchburg, VA 24504
(434) 845-1888
www.amazementsquare.org

Historic Crab Orchard Museum and Pioneer Park
Route 1, P.O. Box 194
Tazewell, VA 24651
(276) 988-6755
www.craborchardmuseum.com

Jamestown Settlement
Jamestown-Yorktown Foundation
P.O. Box 1607
Williamsburg, VA 23187
(888) 593-4682
www.historyisfun.org

MacCallum More Museum and Gardens
603 Hudgins Street
P.O. Box 104
Chase City, VA 23924
(434) 372-0502
www.mmmg.org

Occoneechee State Park Visitor Center
1192 Occoneechee State Park Road
Clarksville, VA 23927
(434) 374-2210
www.dcr.virginia.gov/parks/occoneec

Shenandoah Valley Discovery Museum
54 South Loudoun Street
Winchester, VA 22604
(540) 722-2020
www.discoverymuseum.net

South Boston-Halifax County Museum
P.O. Box 383
1540 Wilborn Avenue
South Boston, VA 24592
(434) 572-9200
www.sbhcmuseum.org

Virginia Department of Transportation
Cultural Preservation Program
www.virginiadot.org/infoservice/prog-cultural-preservation.asp

Virginia's Explore Park
P.O. Box 8508
Roanoke, VA 24014
(540) 427-1800
www.explorepark.org

Virginia Historical Society
P.O. Box 7311
Richmond, VA 23221-0311
(804) 358-4901
www.vahistorical.org

**Virginia Marine Science
Museum**
717 General Booth Boulevard
Virginia Beach. VA 23451
(757) 425-3474
www.vmsm.com

**Virginia Museum of
Natural History**
1001 Douglas Avenue
Martinsville, VA 24112
(276) 666-8600
www.vmnh.net

Additional Resources

Alvord, Clarence W., and Lee Bidgood. 1912. *The first explorations of the trans-Allegheny region by the Virginians, 1650–1674.* Cleveland, OH: Arthur H. Clark. Co.

Benthall, Joseph L. 1969. *Archeological investigation of the Shannon site, Montgomery County, Virginia.* Richmond: Virginia State Library.

Beverly, Robert. 1947. *The history and present state of Virginia.* ed. Louis B. Wright. Chapel Hill: University of North Carolina Press.

Blanton, Dennis B., and Julie A. King, eds. 2004. *Indian and European contact in context: The mid-Atlantic region.* Gainesville: University Press of Florida.

Briceland, Alan Vance. 1987. *Westward from Virginia: The exploration of the Virginia-Carolina frontier, 1650–1710.* Charlottesville: University Press of Virginia.

Cook, Samuel B. 2000. *Monacans and miners. Native American and coal mining communities in Appalachia.* Lincoln: University of Nebraska Press.

Feest, Christian F. 1990. *The Powhatan Indians.* Indians of North America. ed. Frank W. Porter III. New York: Chelsea House Publishers.

Fitzhugh, William F., ed. 1985. *Cultures in contact: The impact of European contacts on Native American cultural institutions, AD 1000–1800.* Washington, DC: Smithsonian Institution Press.

Gardner, William M. 1986. *Lost arrowheads and broken pottery: Traces of Indians in the Shenandoah Valley.* Thunderbird Museum Publication. Manassas, VA: Tru Tone Press.

Gleach, Frederic W. 1997. *Powhatan's world and colonial Virginia.* Lincoln: University of Nebraska Press.

Gunn Allen, Paula. 2004. *Pocahontas: Medicine woman, spy, entrepreneur, diplomat.* San Francisco: HarperCollins.

Haile, Edward W. 1995. *Virginia discovered and described by Captain John Smith 1608.* Map based on Smith and Zuñiga maps. Champlain, VA: Globe Sales Publications.

———. 1996. *England in America: The Chesapeake Bay from Jamestown to St. Mary's City, 1607–1634.* Towns from Smith and Zuñiga maps on modern base map. Richmond, VA: Dietz Press.

———. 1998. *Jamestown narratives: Eyewitness accounts of the Virginia colony: The first decade 1607–1617.* Champlain, VA: Round House.

Hantman, Jeffery L., and Gary Dunham. 1993. The enlightened archaeologist. *Archaeology* (May/June): 44–49.

Harriot, Thomas. 1972. *A Brief and true report of the new found land of Virginia: The complete 1590 Theodor de Bry edition.* New York: Dover Publications, Inc.

Houck, Peter W., and Mintey D. Maxham. 1993. *Indian Island in Amherst County.* Lynchburg, VA: Warwick House Publishing.

Kupperman, Karen O. 2000. *Indians and English: Facing off in early America.* Ithica, NY: Cornell University Press.

Moretti-Langholtz, Danielle. 2002. *In their own words: Voices of Virginia Indians.* Video. Williamsburg, VA: American Indian Resource Center, College of William and Mary.

———. 2003. *In their own words: Voices of Virginia Indians.* Interactive multimedia CD. Williamsburg, VA: American Indian Resource Center, College of William and Mary.

Perdue, Theda. 1989. *The Cherokee.* Indians of North America. ed. Frank W. Porter III. New York: Chelsea House Publishers.

Potter, Stephen R. 1993. *Commoners, tribute, and chiefs: The development of Algonquian culture in the Potomac Valley.* Charlottesville: University Press of Virginia.

Reinhart, Theodore R., and Mary Ellen N. Hodges, eds. 1990. *Early and Middle Archaic research in Virginia: A synthesis.* Special publication 22. Richmond: Archeological Society of Virginia.

———. 1991. *Archaic and Early Woodland research in Virginia: A synthesis.* Special publication 24. Richmond: Archeological Society of Virginia.

———. 1992. *Middle and Late Woodland research in Virginia: A synthesis.* Special publication 25. Richmond: Archeological Society of Virginia.

Rountree, Helen C. 1989. *The Powhatan Indians of Virginia.* Norman: University of Oklahoma Press.

———. 1990. *Pocahontas's people: The Powhatan Indians of Virginia through four centuries.* Norman: University of Oklahoma Press.

———. 1993. *Powhatan foreign relations, 1500–1722.* Charlottesville: University Press of Virginia.

———. 1995. *Young Pocahontas in the Indian world.* Yorktown, VA: J & R Graphic Services.

———. 2005. *Pocahontas, Powhatan, Opechancanough: Three Indian lives changed by Jamestown.* Charlottesville: University Press of Virginia.

Rountree, Helen C., and E. Randolph Turner III. 2002. *Before and after Jamestown: Virginia's Powhatans and their predecessors.* Gainesville: University Press of Florida.

Townsend, Camilla. 2004. *Pocahontas and the Powhatan dilemma.* New York: Hill and Wang.

Trigger, Bruce G., ed. 1978. *Handbook of North American Indians: Northeast,* vol. 15. Washington, DC: Smithsonian Institution Press.

Waugaman, Sandra F., and Danielle Moretti-Langholtz. 2000. *We're still here: Contemporary Virginia Indians tell their stories.* Richmond, VA: Palari Publishing.

Wittkofski, J. Mark, and Theodore R. Reinhart, eds. 1989. *Paleoindian research in Virginia: A synthesis.* Special publication 19. Richmond: Archeological Society of Virginia.

Wood, Karenne, ed. 2007. *The Virginia Indian Heritage Trail.* Charlottesville: Virginia Foundation for the Humanities.

Wood, Peter H., et al., eds. 1990. *Powhatan's mantle: Indians of the colonial southeast.* Lincoln: University of Nebraska Press.

Index